When the Tiger Weeps

BOOKS OF POETRY AND TRANSLATION BY MIKE O'CONNOR

The Rainshadow (1983)

The Basin:
Life in a Chinese Province (1988)

Only a Friend Can Know:
Poems and Translations on the Theme of *Chih-yin* (1997)

Setting Out:
a novel by Tung Nien (1998)

The Clouds Should Know Me by Now:
Buddhist Poet-Monks of China (1998)
(*edited with Red Pine*)

When I Find You Again, It Will Be in Mountains:
Selected Poetry of Chia Tao (779-843) (2000)

Where the World Does Not Follow:
Buddhist China in Picture and Poem (2002)
(*photography by Steven R. Johnson*)

•

ANTHOLOGIES

Working the Woods, Working the Sea:
An Anthology of Northwest Writing (1986)

Paperwork:
Contemporary Poems from the Job (1991)

Frontier Taiwan:
An Anthology of Modern Chinese Poetry (2001)

Mike O'Connor

WHEN
THE
TIGER
WEEPS

Pleasure Boat Studio
A Literary Press

I wish to acknowledge my gratitude to the publishers of the following books for permission to reprint previously published material: Empty Bowl Books: "Song of Ishi," "Elegy for a Log Truck Driver," "Kerouac Creek Work Tune," and "Rainshadow Economics" from *The Rainshadow*; "Kuan-yin Shan: Mother of Mercy Mountain," "Japanese Currents," and "A Bow to You, Bu-wen" from *The Basin: Life in a Chinese Province.* § Pleasure Boat Studio: A Literary Press: Chapter 46 from *Setting Out*, by Tung Nien, translated by Mike O'Connor. § Wisdom Publications: "When the Tiger Weeps," from *Where the World Does Not Follow*; and from *When I Find You Again, It Will Be in Mountains: Selected Poems of Chia Tao (779-843).* § Thanks also to the editors of the following publications where some of the poems and translations for this volume appeared: *Dalmo'ma, Chicago Review, China Times, Bombay Gin, Crosscurrents, Mudlark, Tangram, Two Rivers, Taiwan Travel, Longhouse, International Quarterly, Minotaur,* and *Vigilance.* § "Sakura" was a broadside from Pleasure Boat Studio: A Literary Press.

Illustrations: p. 16 / "Fred Grant and his Father" by Douglas Gorsline, copyright 1971; with permission from Marie Gorsline. § p. 45 / "Ishi /1911," Courtesy of the Phoebe Apperson Hearst Museum of Anthropology and the Regents of the University of California—photographed by Alfred Kroeber, #15-5412 § p. 61 / "Clippings from the sporting news *Esto*," Mexico City. § p. 85 / "Woodcutting up Jimmy-Come-Lately Creek at Bubb Schade's Sacred Alder Grove." Watercolor by the author. § p. 105 / "Clippings from Tienanmen Square," from the *Chung-kuo shih-pao, China Times*, Taipei. § p. 129 / "Children of Datong." Photograph by Steven R. Johnson. § p. 145 /"Traveling among Mountains and Rivers." Painting by Fan K'uan, Sung Dynasty, with permission from the Palace Museum, Taipei.

Cover Art: *The Parallel Universe Series, No. 1,* by Jim Ball
(acrylic, mixed media on canvas— 5' h by 10' w)

Set in Dante
Book design by JB Bryan

ISBN: 1-929355-18-1

Library of Congress Control Number: 2004092921

Pleasure Boat Studio: A Literary Press
201 West 89th St., #6F
New York, NY 10024
Tel-fax (888) 810-5308
email: pleasboat@nyc.rr.com
www.pbstudio.com

LING-HUI

Contents

BOOK TWO

*Orpheus sang his complaints
to the rocks and the mountains,
melting the hearts of tigers and
moving the oaks from their station.*
BULLFINCH'S MYTHOLOGY

BOOK ONE

BOOK ONE

Volunteer Park

I lean back
against this grand old oak
to nap.

Over my head
a few dry copper leaves
rustle on a branch.

Pure spring light
enters
a blade of new grass,

fills it like a cup,
and the soft,
diffused light

(like our lives)

is more beautiful
than if it shined.

ORION'S SWORD
A POEM OF THE AMERICAN CIVIL WAR

To the memory of my Great, Great Grandfather,
Private Samuel D. Breare,
First Brigade, General Banks Division, Maryland

"Now you've enlisted in the army,
so take this road and go—
be like the wind-driven waves
rising on the sea at Kuang-ling."

  —CHIA TAO (779-843)
  "Farewell to a Military Enlistee, on the Road"

"Show me a man who feels bitterly toward
John Brown, and let me hear what noble verse
he can repeat. He'll be as dumb as if his lips were stone."

  —HENRY DAVID THOREAU
  "The Last Days of John Brown"

"In peace I chanted peace,
but now the drum of war is mine."

  —WALT WHITMAN
  "City of Ships" in *Drum Taps*

Monday oct 21 1861

Dear mother

    I take my pen in hand to rite a few lines to you to let you
know that i am well and hopeing you are all the same mother
I was thinking that we was to march to day but we havent
gon yet and we dont expect to go for two or three days we
belong to the first brigade of Banks Division we are
enbanked near Dawsonville the name of our camp is Camp
Linbon we have bin embanked hear about two weeks I roat a
letter to John Thomas and sent a few lines to you by his letter
I roat his letter on the 20th on the 28 of November i will be
listed three months and then i will try and get a furlough and
home and see you if i live that long give my love and best
respects to all my kind friends that is all i have to say at
present

        excuse my bad writing
        hear is a fine map
        we will be pade about the last of this month
        mother

                Your Dear Son,
                Samuel D. Breare

Direct your letter
private Samuel D Breare
in care of Capt J N Taylor
30 rigament henna voluntears
via washington general Banks
Division Maryland

[Note: According to family history, Sam Breare was fifteen or sixteen years of age when he penned the above letter. Among other duties, he served as water boy for his regiment, and, in fact, got himself wounded one evening on a river bank by sniper fire while hauling water to his camp.]

Introductory Note

This poem narrates the journey Ulysses S. Grant made from Nashville to Washington D.C. in the spring of 1864 to be confirmed as lieutenant-general, a newly revived rank, that would give him command of all the armies of the Union. Most major historians have Grant boarding the train in Nashville and getting off in Washington, but the four-day journey itself was never documented.

In addition to the train journey, a second timeline of the poem presents the major battles and events that inevitably resulted from Grant's coming East. A third element of the poem is the chorus (various voices) making comments and observations about Grant as the poem, the train, rolls along.

March 4th, 1864

So Grant, his eldest son, 14,
and two staff officers
get on the train at Nashville in the morning.

The night before,
with War Department orders just received,
Grant wrote, "I will not stay in Washington,"
to Sherman, who thinks the politicians there
more dangerous than a battlefield.

•

Already
musket-shattered trees
of the Wilderness—
oak, sweet gum and pine,
with an underbrush of skeletons
and eyeless skulls—
are blossoming again
with smoke and fire.

•

Under a sky half cloud, half blue,
Grant's car flashes
intermittently with sun.
He lights a fresh cigar,
clamps it in his teeth, leans back.

His service uniform's worn and faded;
his frame, when he shuffles down the aisle,
slightly stooped.
At every stop, his chief of staff
hands him new dispatches
his dark gray eyes digest.

> "He looks more like a subaltern
> than a general. Slouchy. Rumpled.
> And wasn't he drunk
> when he fell from a borrowed mount,
> dislocating a hip,
> on leave near New Orleans?"

But Lincoln's got it right:
"Unconditional-Surrender" Grant
has bagged two armies and licked a third;
thus on him now devolves
command of all the armies.
"He makes things git," said Lincoln.

•

On an oak ridge in the East,
Lee, astride his famous horse,
senses in the colored western clouds
more than a subtle change of weather;
senses (and suspects, in fact, from spies
in Washington) the storm
that will be bursting on Virginia;

the menace,
coming at him from the West,
clickity-clack,
and wonders grimly if it's true
of Grant what wasn't
true of Lincoln's other generals,
that "once he gets his teeth in,
he won't let go."

●

The wood-fed steam locomotive
carries Grant and staff into Kentucky:
the late-winter land
not yet green with beech and gum;
a few hardscrabble farms and cabins,
a grist mill with a turning water-wheel.

  "If Grant comes East, across the mountains,
  he'll bring more death
    than poor Cassandra ever sang,
    or Sherman, in a fit, divined."

An hour out of Louisville,
Grant's train passes
into bluegrass parklands,
and later, in the Burly,
he spots tobacco barns
not yet filled with leaf.

"He didn't like serving
in the Mexican War;
he drank too much
when posted on the Coast;
he peddled firewood
on the streets of St. Louis;
collected bills;
ended up clerking
at his father's harness shop.
He also finished 27th
in his West Point class, while Lee,
in his, was second; he once believed
his calling: water colorist;
and now—defying horse sense—
he'll hold the rank George Washington once held
and direct 600,000 men in war?"

•

"We're tenting on the old Camp ground . . . ."
The Army of the Potomac moves;
and with its 3,500 wagons,
29,000 horses and 20,000 mules,
from camps near Culpeper
and Brandy Station,
crosses the upper Rapidan
and runs into a brick wall,
Lee—muzzle to muzzle—
at the Wilderness.

17,000 Union casualties,
and yet the soldiers cheer
when Grant retreats—Grant-fashion—
not back across the Rapidan
with the ambulance trains,
but on to Spotsylvania,
and the Bloody Angle,
six-to-eight dead bodies deep
before the Rebel breastworks,
and the Union loses 20,000 more
(and a forest)
and marches on through flame and smoke
—Grant-fashion—
to the swamps and sluggish streams
around Cold Harbor, feeling for,
then pounding at, the Rebel right;

and there, by the Chickahominy River,
7,000 Northern soldiers die
in less than seven minutes,
"dying on the old Camp ground."
("Not war," someone pronounced, "but murder.")
An assault that gave Grant grief
and long regret.

     "I've heard Grant's got
     presidential ambitions."

     "Grant don't like nothin'
     but smokin' and fightin'."

The army disengages,
crosses the Chickahominy,
and in a brilliant turning movement
steals a march on Lee,
sideslipping to the wide James River
just ahead.

•

The train whistles at each crossing,
where, now and then,
a mule-drawn wagon waits
on a crushed-limestone road.

Near Christianburg—after stopping
to take on wood and water—Grant,
the touted horseman, spots
a handsome thoroughbred
the cavalry somehow overlooked.

•

After two days in the "iron storm"
of Second Wilderness,
Sheridan, alone brought East by Grant,
cuts loose on his big proud horse,
rides hell-bent along with Custer
around Lee's army, kills Jeb Stuart,
and rides (all 115 pounds of him)
like Hotspur to the Union lines.

Soon, Sheridan, armed
with repeating carbine,
will mount again
his battle charger,
winning big at Winchester,
Fisher's Hill and, in that famous ride,
at Cedar Creek; annihilating two armies,
laying waste the Shenandoah Valley
so that "a crow flying over
need carry its own provisions";
and he will slash again at Petersburg
and outrun Lee to Lynchburg for checkmate.

•

As the train nears Frankfort,
dusk settles over fallow wheat
and Indian corn fields.
The iron horse, in an outpouring of whistles
and thick smoke, stops
at the little capital
and, after Georgetown with its college
(and after the grade school Grant attended)
turns sharply north.

  "Let's face it: Lincoln's just an undertaker;
  he doesn't mind Grant's drinking
  if he'll do the killing for him.
  The names are interchangeable:
  Lincoln, Grant, the Devil,

though I dare say
that isn't fair to the Devil."

"But surely emancipation
of the slave justifies, nay, even
ennobles this war."

"Lincoln, Grant, the Devil."

•

The army of a hundred thousand men
takes four days to cross the tidal James
on a 2000-foot span improvised by engineers
not matched since Xerxes' Greek invasion.

And then, surprising Lee,
Grant lays siege to Petersburg—
rail and manufacturing center—
instead of Richmond.

The labyrinthine Confederate
entrenchments run 53 miles
with abatis, palisades—
those hellish pointed stakes
with the French name: *chevaux-de-frise*—
and enclosed forts with guns.

After months inside
this terrible crescent,

Lee's men are close to famine,
with one Confederate soldier
(many boys as young as Grant's
son Frederick; many old men, too)
spaced every fifteen feet
within their self-dug graves,
and stretching.

•

Grant's train runs through
leafless apple orchards past Cynthiana,
clickity-clack, Williamstown, Dry Ridge
to the broad Ohio River,
where Grant looks out
the window of the dining car
on Cincinnati
(the name of his big bay horse)
where his party finds a hotel
for the night. (His other horse
answers to Jeff Davis.)
Clickity-clack.

•

Deep in the South,
the Confederacy takes a wound in the gut:
Atlanta, with its warehouses, hotels,
boarding rooms, private homes, hospitals, churches,
arsenals, shops, schools, taverns, and depots,
no longer exists—

lone chimneys rake the sky,
mark ash and ruin.

Atlanta fallen, Atlanta burned
so grizzled-bearded Sherman
(a hawk-nosed Moses to the Blacks;
a John Brown back from the gallows
of Harper's Ferry,
all business this time, brother,
with an army 60,000 strong)
soars victorious, an eagle
in shining clouds; and
soon to learn of Andersonville,
chews like a wolf at Georgia's carcass;
marches his mighty army to the sea.
And all over the state,
thousands of slaves cast off their manacles
and slip away from cotton farms and burned plantations,
seeking haven in the Union lines. An exodus
momentous as that
from the affliction of a Pharaoh—
for "The Lord is my strength and my song."

•

The train winds oblivious through the night
under pale evening stars;
Frederick, cupping his hands
against the window,
spies Orion, tells Grant,
who asks, "Does he have his sword?"

And Grant
takes out a map
of North Virginia and
spreads it on his knees,
puzzles for a while
(that squinty left eye)
while Frederick asks,
"Is that where Lee lives?"

•

And Grant, looking toward
the works of Petersburg,
summons Sheridan and says,
"I now feel like ending the matter."

•

The rocking of the racketing car
rocks Grant to sleep.
"Meekness and grimness meet in him,"
wrote Melville.
Clickity-clack.

"Is there an element of ignorance here
or just a missing quality of imagination?
There's something peculiar in him, sure."
As Sherman said, "To me he is a mystery,
And I believe he is a mystery to himself."

Whatever the wellspring of his power,
he has none of the peacock,
none of the officer's strut.

And he's clear-headed under fire;
has been seen leaning against a tree,
calmly whittling with his knife while
armies clash around him in the night."

•

And the entrenched Confederates
in their ninth month under siege,
in their ninth month of suffering
dawn and dusk bombardments from the Federals;
brave beyond words, malnourished and ill-shod,
hold to the slimmest hope:
to flee and join Joe Johnston,
then go wreck Sherman in the Carolines.

•

The train rumbles on: Pennsylvania,
the Appalachian Ridge and Valley Region,
Maryland, passes white-washed churches,
farms with just a sign of ploughing underway;
crosses trestled rivers
in the rosy dawn;
rolls on implacably,
trailing its long black plume of smoke.

"If he's just firm
in the right, as the Lord gives him
to see the right . . .
inexplicable, deep, dark and
winding like a river . . . ."

"You might as well
accept it . . . he won't scare."

      •

And irrepressible Sheridan
on that big black horse,
flamboyant Custer with his golden locks,
go busting, smashing into Five Forks;
and Grant signals an assault
all along the lines,
and Petersburg's defenses fall;
and Richmond shortly after.

Lincoln, unguarded, striding ashore
to spend the night,
finds, to his deep embarrassment,
Richmond's former slaves
hailing him as Christ.

      •

In peaceful, prosperous Maryland,
the long white fences

enclose horse pasture,
neat and pampered
as rolling lawns. The train
jerks to a stop at Baltimore,
then creeps on.
(Grant, in fact, could use a drink,
if Puritanical Rawlins, chief of staff,
would permit him;
if Frederick—his mother's
eyes and loyal subject—
would permit him.)

A mile beyond the switchyards,
cherry trees show flecks of blossom,
the ground beneath, a trace of snow.

Getting closer to the capital,
to Lincoln, whom he's never met
but thinks well of (another Westerner)
and knows that all he asks is "fight";
getting closer to the whirlwind
that he must feed with bloodshed
and constrain,

Grant puts out the stub of his cigar
in the silver spittoon on the floor,
and Frederick gathers up
his father's bulky carpet bag.

•

Across a broad and dusty field
near Appomattox,
a dove is flying
where a rebel rides:
it is a white flag fluttering
at the end of a staff,
carried by that rebel riding—
and quiet falls like dusk
upon the battlefield.
And with his army come apart,
Lee, the good King Arthur
of the worst of causes,
in his last dress uniform
and ceremonial sword,
"would rather die a thousand deaths
than go see Grant,"
but goes.

●

At Washington, late afternoon,
a whistle pierces somber air;
60-inch locomotive drive-wheels
brake and slow
on the straight tracks,
and shoot out steam.

A release of stack smoke
billows to the station's roof.

The platform's filled
with local soldiers and civilians.

But due to an official mix up,
no one's there to meet him,
"this man
who even in a crowd
seems all alone."

When Grant,
in unbuttoned military coat,
steps off the train into the cold,
the war ends.

Coda I

"(Arous'd and angry, I'd thought to beat the alarum,
                              and urge relentless war,
But soon my fingers fail'd me, my face droop'd
                              and I resign'd myself,
To sit by the wounded and soothe them,
                              or silently watch the dead)"

—WALT WHITMAN
"The Wound-Dresser" in *Drum Taps*

Coda II

Telegraph to Secretary of War Stanton,
dated 4:30 P.M., April 9, 1865:

General Lee surrendered the Army of Northern Virginia this
afternoon on terms proposed by myself. The accompanying
additional correspondence will show the conditions fully.

Signed: U.S. Grant
Lieutenant-General

When word of peace
goes out
from Appomattox
across the battlefield
and skirmish lines,
though Grant had ordered
no salute of guns,
the soldiers of the Army,
camp by camp,
break into cheers,
hug and kiss each other
and throw—"hurrah! hurrah!"—
their caps and coats,
into the spring Virginia air.

When word of peace
goes out from Appomattox,

it travels west to Lynchburg
where General Meade, old "snapping turtle,"
gets off his horse to cheer
among his cheering men,
"It's over boys, it is all over."

Word travels east to Farmville
and Burkes Station
and it is passed to Jetersville,
Amelia Courthouse,
and farther east to shattered Petersburg
and burned-out Richmond
with its tolling bells.

And where it reaches
camp bands play
and Yankees cheer and cry,
and throw their hats and coats
into the softly drizzling air
and throw their threadbare blankets, too,
and muskets and canteens—
a contagious joy-filled demonstration
repeated fifty miles
across the dogwood-dotted land.

•

Then all the jubilance
and animation stop.
Those caps and coats

tossed in exuberance freeze
suspended in mid-air.
The pine wood landscape drains
of color, and a roar of clouds
sends cold black rain
sweeping over soldiers
as over stone.

•

A nine-car funeral train,
Locomotive 331, draped in black cloth
and crepe, creeps and chuffs
out of Washington Station
with a crowd of mourners on the platform
and hundreds of dignitaries aboard,
departing for Springfield, Illinois,
with the coffins and bodies
of Lincoln, and his son Will,
whose death at eleven,
over time, unbalanced Mary Lincoln.

The train picks up steam,
("O Captain! My Captain!")
heading out through a relentless rain
(Washington black in muslin,
New York a sea of mourners
from the Battery to Central Park),
heading out through black farmland,
black ranging hills

and black-draped cities,
over thirteen railroads
to a grieving people,
where, when the train stops or passes,
whole towns turn out and line the tracks
and kneel.

"He was incontestably the greatest man
I've ever known," said U.S. Grant.

And this was, fittingly,
the largest funeral
in all of history.

•

Then, almost as suddenly
as the bullet-rain and darkness
befell the land,
a flood of light and color return.

The White House flag
tops the staff again
as victorious armies
under a cloudless sky
march twelve abreast
down Pennsylvania Avenue
in two days of Grand Review;
and the largest crowd
ever to descend on Washington

sings to the marching,
chants "John Brown's Body,"
and a host of patriotic songs.
Women weep, babies
and old men wave tiny flags,
young girls strew flowers
in the path of the proud
tramping armies—
blinding bayonet glitter
from the mass of infantry;
a storm of hoof beats
from seven miles of cavalry,
and Sherman's army alone,
with its long-striding, hardy
Westerners, taking six hours
to pass the review stand,
as at last the Federal Armies,
200,000 men or more, march in glory
out of existence.

•

Then the clock turns back,
and it's springtime in Virginia,
and those hats and coats,
hurled in euphoria and suspended
in mid-air, rise and fall again,
as songs of regimental bands
resume from camp to camp.
And the soldiers in the field,
no longer locked in war

("that feast of vultures and the waste of life"),
no longer circled by
Death's dark angels,
look about themselves
in wonderment, and,
with new eyes, drink in
the redbud blossoming
landscape of Virginia.

And it is spring for real,
the most memorable
in all their lives.

SONG OF ISHI

When Blue Jay Goes to Bed

Smoke from a tended fire
curls above a brush shelter
in the madrone trees.

A woman with baby and basket
calls to the man fishing
waist-deep in the Yuna River.

Grandmother looks up
from her bead work;

Elder looks up
from his arrow-making.

The last light is rose on the volcano—
and now falls the wing of a crow.

Words of a Yahi Tribesman

I hate to leave this river
and the hills my people love.
Who are these strangers
who bring us sickness, war and death?

Spirit, my people have listened
to your presence:
      in the laughter of salmon's river,
       in the rustling leaves of crow's pine.

You know the joy
      the acorn's ripeness brings,
      the delight the tiny huckleberry holds.

Oak, scrub pine and lush meadows . . .
I am dizzy with ignorance.
You know what I can't know,
      see what I can't see;

but even though the stars over the western ocean
      should one
      by one
        go out . . .

Rapid as We Vanish

My digging stick I break
and take up the hunting bow.
Yesterday at the caves,
six of our people gunned down in surprise.
Whiteman is more driven
than the spawning salmon.
What evil comes upon this land
swifter than a cloud covering the moon?

Now we place a rock cairn to mark
our people's place. Now,
and everywhere,
    the cropped heads of our mourning women
       —like uncovered wild bulbs—
      rapid as we vanish,

      appear.

Song of Ishi

To breast the swift river
on a hot clear day;
to rope-climb a towering
canyon wall;
stalk, gut and skin
the beautiful deer;
pound up acorn
into meal.

At feast time after harvest,
I am crazy with love.
In winter, I make a new bow.

Caught in a rainstorm,
buckskin keeps my fire drill dry.

Hare snare for small fishing;
double prong poon for the salmon.

Eagle, buzzard, blue jay
feather my arrows;
tail of a wildcat
to put them in.

Children, mush and lots of singing;
strike of a rattler; flick of a bowstring.

Waganupa foothill wilderness,
years ago.

Ishie Shantie

Sitshum skookum chuck
kopa hyas waum klah sun;
lope klatawa sagalie hyas tall
tanino skookum kullah;
mamook hunt, mamook gut pe mamook skin
kloshe mowitch;
kokshut tukwilla
kopa sapolil.

Kopa hiyu muckamuck kimtah iskum sapolil
nika pelton kopa ticky.
Cole illahee nika mamook chee opitlkegh.

Kopa hiyu snass
man mowitch skin kloshe nanitch nika piah stick.

Kwitshadie lepiege kopa tenas pish;
lapushet kopa sammon.

Chakchak, buzzard, spooh kalakala
tupso nika kalitan;
opoots hyas pusspuss
mahsh klaska kopa.

Hiyu tenas, mush pe hiyu shantie;
shugh opoots pight elip; opitlkegh tenas lope latlah.

Waganupa lepee tenas saghalie illahee lemolo illahee
ahnkuttie.

Late Winter Dream Song

Over the smoke hole
rides the last snow moon.
A spring wind retrieves the rain.

Even now I can picture
the salmon flashing
in the sun-lit streams
and the tender clover
bursting through the rock.

Arrow whizzing from a new drawn bow:
        fresh deer meat!
I will dance and sing for six days!

Summer

Sleeping rattlesnake, it's too hot to strike.
Cool tastes the pounded manzanita.
We fish in the early morning hours,
swim in the afternoon.
Learn the stars in the open night sky,
go to Waganupa, to the shade
of her slopes and tall trees.

Hunting summer fat deer,
     hunting the breeze.

Rattle Song

Fawn cry, arrow whiz,
snake rattle, coyote yip,
water fall, timber creak,
fire crackle, wind pine roar.

Grizzly growl, dove moan,
insect buzz, raven call,
    stone flake click,
        fire drill whirr,
rain drip, squirrel squeak,

    bare foot steps.

Down from the Hills

Long ago I left off hiding.
Twelve of us were a nation;
five of us were a nation—
I alone am nothing left.

Old Coyote Doctor, you can't hurt me now.
The bones of my people are scattered like chaparral
    through the foothills.
Yuna Creek is as blank as a night of snow.
The last deer has gone to the volcano.
Little rabbit, I would rather starve than kill you.
Old Coyote Doctor, you can't hurt me now.
Loneliness was your best arrow:
sharper than hunger, more accurate than fear.
I'm tired now.
I have crossed the boundary of my people's land
and the boundary of Coyote Night.

In the east, beyond that stick corral,
where Whiteman's dogs
are barking an alarm,

            that rose in the heavens
            must be the dawn.

Ishi in Town

A plane is nothing when you see the Hawk.
Don't feel bad, but a skyscraper
            is a poor mountain.
      I like this penny whistle very much,
but it won't call rabbits.
            Whiskey is amber as upper Mill Creek,
      but it's crazy fire.
I must hold my laughing sides
            when I see typewriter.
      Old Salmon leaps up rapids
      a boat can't float down,

      but all in all
      I like these pockets
      in my pants.

You Stay, I Go

"Everybody hoppy?"
March 25th, 1916,
the last wild Indian of America is dead.
Tubercle bacillus—
like an arrow to his lung.

"Everybody hoppy?"
Yahi-Medicine-Old-Man Kuwi,
keep Coyote Doctor from our door.

Like an arrow to his lung—
and smoke to the four directions
can't cure him,
can't suck out the pain.

"Do you believe in God?"
"Sure, Mike."

And his spirit flies the burning body
        to the Land of the Dead,
where the oak, scrub pine and lush meadows
    whisper his secret name,

        to the Land of the Dead,
where sidewalks, trolley cars and playgrounds
            whisper his secret name . . .

    Ishi having crossed all the Realms.

Thinking of Ishi While Reading the Want Ads

Hairstylist
Furnace Installer
Jobs! Jobs! Jobs!
Data Processor
Nickel Alloy Machinist
Daily Delivery, Monday thru Sunday
Are You an Elephant? Why Work for Peanuts?
Hunter/Gatherer
Activist Minded? Use Our Phone Bank.
Taxi Driver. Must Have Washington License.

Ishi and the Braves

He wouldn't have been insulted
by the war chants or the "chop":
he wouldn't have understood them!

Nation, tribe wiped out
when he'd only known how many springs;
and you don't throw a tomahawk
at salmon or deer.

But he would have been interested in,
and nervous of, the crowd,
just as he had been more curious
about the audience at the vaudeville show,
Berkeley, 1912, than about the show itself.

He knew people, but he didn't know groups.

The ball game under the great lights
of the stadium in Atlanta, Georgia
would have played on below him,
a sideshow of jugglers and clowns
as against the spectacle of 60 thousand
cheering, demonstrative Atlantans.

"More people than stars," he might have mused.

•

The multi-millionaire slugger
pulls a high fastball screaming
toward the left-field stands
right at Ishi,
and the hunter-gatherer of Yuna Creek,
surprised, shoots up his arm
and nails it on the fly.

The multitudinous Atlantans
seeing this directly,
or on the wide outfield monitor,
explode with happiness,
believing that this squat,
middle-aged Indian, now standing
before them, still holding the ball,
is the promotional genius of baseball
and not, in a million years,
the "last wild Indian" of America.

·

"Atlanta is ours and fairly won,"
General William Tecumseh Sherman,
in a wire to Abraham Lincoln,
September 2, 1862,
two days before Sherman's army
burned Atlanta to the ground.

CANCIÓN DEL CORDOBÉS

Don Felix (Spain, 1936)

Life was very good for Don Felix
till the socialist-anarchist rabble
seized his olive-rich land:
forty thousand acres,
and a thousand Satillo brave bulls.

The town was heady with reform;
the town was rife with anarchy;
churches burned while mobs of workers
sang the "Internationale."
So Don Felix, with some of his family,
got in his imported car
and fled to the Nationalist lines,
to his palace in Seville.

With Don Felix out of the picture,
the poor folk of Palma del Rio
killed hundreds of beautiful bulls.
Never had the town so feasted!
Never had so many tasted
their first boiled steak!

When the fascists retook the town,
the town they called Palma the Red,
a vengeful Don Felix
shot half the men in the pueblo—
"Ten men for every slain bull,"
is what the aristocrat said.

But Don Felix made the church bells ring
again, and put the peasants back to work.
Order and hunger returned to the town,
and Don Felix returned to his land:
forty thousand acres of olives
and still hundreds of bulls for a herd.

Winter of Triumph (Mexico, 1964) / *El Grunudo*

At the beginning of the 1964 bullfight season in Mexico, everyone agreed the greatest matador was Paco Camino. The critics loved his classical style. That he was brave was beyond question, but he was also graceful and artistic. What is more, he was very handsome, and he had recently married the rich and beautiful daughter of the owner of the largest bull fight arena in the world, the Plaza Mexico. He fought very well that season but critics and *aficionados* remarked that he stayed farther away from the bulls' horns than was customary—at least until Mexico was on the threshold of replacing him in their hearts with El Cordobés.

Not many had heard of El Cordobés when the season began. A Spaniard born of Andalucian peasant stock in the village of Palma del Rio in 1934, or two years before the start of the Spanish Civil War, he was now in his late twenties, rather old to be getting started in the profession. At first, the critics ate him for lunch. He was awkward, even clumsy and, perhaps most irritating to conservatives, he had a mop of hair fuller than that of a Beatle. In fact, he was dubbed El Beatle, or alternately, *El Grunudo* (matted hair). He was handsome in a rugged way (he bore a resemblance to Robert Kennedy) and was a bachelor. He could not read or write.

In the ring, he often was the source of amusement, talking to the bulls, sitting down in front of them, petting them on their muzzles. But the amusement was always mixed with awe for his bravery and a degree of fear for him. He worked so close to the horns that it was often painful to watch him. Like only a few other matadors, he preferred to place the *banderillos* himself rather than have one of the *caudrilla*, or specialists, do it. But unlike other matadors or *banderilleros*, he liked to break the sticks in half before placing them, thereby doubling the danger by shortening the distance between himself and the horns. He also liked to place the shortened sticks while first standing with his back to the bull, inciting it to charge rather than running at it. Many critics called him crazy; others, very brave. In a fairly short time, however, his courage won over most of the public, and they began to see that his art, while somewhat ragged in technique, had everything of great and genuine emotion.

Paco Camino had a very good season that year, but only as the second or third best matador in Mexico. Joselita Huerta, for instance, also had a very big Mexico tour that year. El Cordobés by a great margin out-fought the field, Mexican, Spanish and Latin American. A few months later back in Madrid, the matador suffered a near-fatal goring by an enormous bull nearly blind in one eye called Impulsivo. But El Cordobés fought again within the month, and though he would be gored as many as twenty times in his career, he survived to become one of the greatest matadors in the history of the *corrida*. Retired and wealthy, he still lives in Spain. His son, also called El Cordobés, now fights the bulls.

Good Seats

At our first bull fights, *corrida de toros*, my friend Brian and I sat in the cheapest, highest seats in the Plaza Mexico, the largest bull arena in the world. Being from the Northwest, we were happy to have the seats in the sun, *anandas del sol*. Not knowing much about bullfights or the Mexican sun, we enjoyed being among the more colorful, animated and poorer elements of Mexico. Everyone up on the rim of the plaza dressed in farm clothes, cowboy hats and sombreros. There were even chickens and dogs with us up there, and lots of wine and beer, and things freshly cooked. Like a farm picnic.

But after we had been initiated into the bullfight and had begun to understand many of the finer points, not to mention identifying with certain matadors, we gradually moved down the plaza levels to near the middle rows. There the men and women were casually urban dressed. Soon, that location wasn't sufficient either. We began to keep our eyes open for the no-shows in the reserved seats, *barrera de sombra*, in the first few rows. We noted how a few others managed to slip into vacant seats once a bullfight had officially begun. Sometimes the upper-class fight-goers—the men dressed in sport coats, suits and ties with the women dressed smartly as well—would shame an individual who tried to upgrade his or her seat near them. We were lucky. On one hand, we looked like nice well-groomed college kids, which we mostly were. We also looked like Americans. Though we might receive inquiries or questioning glances from the aristocrats in the neighboring seats, we were usually given tacit approval for our seat-snatching once our nationality and student-status were established. Mexicans thought it was *muy interesante* that we should be *aficionados*, albeit junior ones; it flattered them a little. And, after all, Catholic Mexico was still deeply mourning the recent assassination of our former President John F. Kennedy and was very sympathetic toward us. In our experience, Mexicans were infallibly kind and friendly hosts; and to be able each Sunday to sit in the best seats of the Plaza Mexico, we were prepared to exploit their good nature.

Brave Heart, Wooden Sword

*"Among working-class boys, this longing to go to the bull
is so agonizingly strong that it makes them risk death."*
—Federico GARCÍA LORCA

The *torero-banderillero* had just placed the third and last pair of
colored, steel-pointed *banderillos* in the withers of the bull
and, to enthusiastic applause, had withdrawn to the shelter-
ing plank barrier, or *burladero*. The bull, now on the opposite
side of the arena, stood uncertainly watching the *banderillero's*
exit. El Cordobés, inside the corral wall, or *barrera*, was
preparing his sword and *muleta* for the third and final phase
of the fight. Suddenly, far across the plaza from us, a young
boy, carrying a wooden sword and a red cloth, jumped from
the first row of seats into the passageway behind the corral
wall and then clambered over it into the arena. The crowd
gasped; and the bull picked out the boy immediately. Guards
had started after the boy, but lacking *torero* experience,
stopped at the wooden fence. One *torero* hurried into the
arena waving a large cape to catch the bull's attention, but
the bull took no notice. At a distance of twenty feet from the
bull, the boy took up position, hooked the wooden sword in
the cloth, and gave the bull a small trembling target. The
helpless plaza held its breath.

The bull charged and the boy stood his ground. At the
moment of imminent death, the bull chose the red cloth, but
swept past so closely that its flanks bowled the boy over and
sent cloth and sword flying. A tumultuous *Ole!* stuck in
everyone's throat. The bull turned to charge again, but the
boy had scrambled to his feet and was running for the safety
of the *barrera*. He might not have made it but for the *torero's*

large cape finally catching the eye of the bull. The boy ran straight into the arms of El Cordobés, who had come out several yards into the ring. He hung onto the matador with all his strength, while El Cordobés, with his signature big grin, held the boy and affectionately tousled his hair, then looked up at the crowd. Everyone rose and gave the pair a tumultuous ovation as the brass band struck up.

Note: It is obviously highly dangerous as well as illegal to jump into the middle of a bull fight. It is not just dangerous for the amateur but for everyone in the ring. Still, there are a number who try it during any one season of fighting. The hope of the *espontaneo* is to take over the bull for a few moments and demonstrate to the crowd that he is worthy of becoming a matador. El Cordobés would know. He did it many times in Spain and was arrested repeatedly for doing it. Before becoming an *espontaneo*, El Cordobés was fighting the brave bulls at night with his friend Juan Horrilla, using his sister's blanket for a *muleta*, in the pastures of the great landowners and bull raisers of Andalucia. The *vaqueros* and Guardia Civil proved more harmful to the young boy than the bulls. He was beaten many times and banished twice from his hometown.

Slaughterhouse

I don't remember the matador's name (it is just as well), but he had fought his second bull skillfully and could expect to cut an ear. The bull was large and his horns, too, but only medium aggressive, medium brave. The matador managed, though, to coax several fine natural passes from him and now, with little hope of coaxing more, was sighting along his sword for the kill. It had taken only a few flicks of his *muleta* to get the bull to stand with his two feet together in proper alignment. The matador, in "the moment of truth," went in over the horns and drove the sword in high up between the bull's shoulder blades. The sword struck bone and sprang out of the bull into the air. The curse of hitting bone happened occasionally to the best of matadors, but it rightfully reduces the chances the matador has of being awarded.

This matador went in just as bravely a second time, but again struck a shoulder blade, the accursed sword bending violently with the pressure of the matador's thrust, then springing, *whanging* into the air. The matador, with a new sword, prepared a third attempt, but when he went in, the bull looked up an inch or so from the *muleta* and just missed hooking the matador's groin. The sword fell to the ground and the bull, turning in frustration, ended standing directly over the instrument of death.

At this point, the crowd could contain itself no longer and began hooting, whistling and booing. The matador had lost all chance of award, and stood now to reap maximum derision from the plaza. On the fourth try, with another new sword, the matador stayed artlessly out of range of the horns, and virtually hurled the sword from several running steps away. Ugly as it was, he managed to get the blade a third of the way in, not deep enough for a kill, but deep enough to stagger the bull and start him coughing up a rivulet of blood. The bull struggled to keep his feet, but with the sword dangling gruesomely from his back, he swayed and stumbled to his knees. The crowd was now beside itself with wrath and indignation. *Aficiones* began hurling cushions, hundreds of cushions, down into the ring at the matador. The matador's hand had been injured by one of the sword-to-bone thrusts and he was trying to hold it and dodge cushions. Two of the *peones* came out from behind the *barrera*, one with a cape to catch and hold the eye of the bull, and the other with a short knife, a *puntilla*, to dispatch the beast. With the flopping of the cape riveting the attention of the bull, the specialist with the knife jabbed quickly but inaccurately. The bull lurched horribly to his feet, the sword still hanging from his shoulders and tried to charge the man who held the *puntilla*, but his legs turned to water under him. More cushions rained into the plaza along with Coca-Cola and beer bottles. The whole stadium was whistling like a sky of hawks in a shrill, menacing chorus. Finally, to the relief of the tens of thousands present—the specialist knocked the sword free from the bull, and with his knife, hit the right spot on the spinal column. The bull received the blow as if electrocuted and lurched over dead.

Another Plaza Attraction

Down in the arena, the team of mules was dragging the dead bull away, when the couple emerged from the third-level passageway. The man was wearing an expensive suit, sunglasses, and had his hair freshly slicked back. He was handsome in a gangster-movie kind of way. On his arm, was an attractive, seductive-looking woman in a very tight dress and too much make-up. They were looking for seats in the section where my friend Brian and I were sitting, but they had come late (the carcass being dragged across the sand was the third of six bulls on the program). The couple could not spot seats, and they caused just enough distraction to receive attention. In fact, you couldn't really *not* notice them. Someone near us shouted their way. Brian and I assumed someone had found them seats. Then someone else shouted *"puta,"* whore, and many people turned their heads to see. *"Puta, puta,"* others shouted. Soon, the couple had the eyes of the whole plaza on them—including those of the *toreros* down in the ring. Those shrill, jeering whistles, usually reserved for matadors who kill badly or fail to kill promptly, filled the plaza; then cushions began to sail into our section. The woman, managing a smile, deflected several cushions before receiving one in the back of the head. The man, angered and grim-faced, shook his fist and cursed the crowd, and received a thrown beer bottle in the back. Finally, he took the woman by the arm and led her away.

A Bad Outing

The Peruvian matador was one of a few South Americans
taking part in the Mexican tour. He had fought without
fanfare that afternoon under an overcast sky in a light drizzle
that had dampened the sand in the arena. The plaza was
barely half full and the spectators wore coats against the chill.
When the wind gusted, it was hard not to pray that the
matador would dispatch the bull as quickly as possible. The
matador, however, was intent on passing the bull once or
twice more, partly to further tire it and get its head down,
and partly to try one last time to elicit some expression of
emotion from the crowd. What was to come felt inevitable.
There were no name fighters here. The crowd, as stated, was
small. The weather was lousy. It was, finally, the wind lifting
the *muleta* on a natural pass that diverted the attention of the
bull and caused him to hook his right horn into the
Peruvian's thigh and lift him like a child's doll into the air.
The *toreros* rushed out and, using their big capes, drew the
bull away from the gored matador, now immobile on the
sand. As the *peones* carried him away to the infirmary under
the stadium—it was not, fortunately, a life-threatening or
career-ending *coronado*—an unseasonable stinging rain began
to fall, and everyone scampered for the exits. The rain was
washing on the bloodied black shoulders of the bull where
the picador had piked him and where the colored *banderillas*
still hung from his withers like ribs of a large kite or broken
fan. Few stayed to see him killed.

Ears and Tail

Late one Sunday afternoon, Marta, the daughter of Senor
and Senora Erdman, at whose home I was staying while in
Mexico City, knocked on the door of my room where I was
studying. Marta was the *afición* of the family. Several years
older than I, attractive, and, alas, married, she couldn't
restrain herself trying to interest me in the bullfight. I had
gone to two fights and neither had produced much feeling in
me nor, apparently, in the spectators. But Marta had urged
me to try again, and especially to go see El Cordobés. "He
looks so much like a Beatle," she said, laughing. When I
finally took her advice, I returned home a convert to the
corrida.

It had been several weeks now that Marta and I had been
sharing an enthusiasm for El Cordobés and the bulls, when
she came knocking on my door, whispering Miguel! Miguel!
Something *muy importante*! I opened the door, and she told
me that El Cordobés had fought in another city that day and
had fought magnificently with a bull so brave that the mata-
dor had asked permission of the president of the *fiesta de los
toros* to set it free. It had been so granted, but because it was
such a very rare occurrence, it was seen by the matador's
detractors as an act of great presumption. It was also sus-
pected by some critics that by the matador's apparent act of
magnanimity and compassion, El Cordobés had managed to
preserve the glory of his indisputably brilliant performance
that afternoon. In effect, they were saying he had neatly side-
stepped the dangerous duty of killing the bull, the phase of
the bullfight in which El Cordobés, and many modern

bullfighters, shined least. Nonetheless, it was reported that the great majority of the spectators expressed strong approval of the act of commutation, and had stood for a long time cheering both matador and brave bull. In the sports papers the next day, several bullfight critics groused about how El Cordobés, "brave but artless," was getting a little too big for his "suit of lights." But for Marta, me and others, who were wholly in the camp of this outrageously brave and long-haired Spaniard, the news was exciting. The brave bull had gone free, and El Cordobés had cut the ears and tail of his critics.

¡El Magnífico!

It was the last bull of the day, and El Cordobés began the *faena*, the fight's third and final act; standing with *muleta* and sword beside the red *barrera*, where, with no room for exit, a matador can be pinned like a butterfly to the wall. The beautiful 1100-kilo bull, bloodied on his shoulders and with six colored *banderillos* hanging from his withers, charged without hesitation the red cloth and thundered by El Cordobés; turned, and charged past again. This was what the crowd had been waiting for. Now the matador tried the pass from his knees, and the bull complied, turned in a clattering of *banderilloes*, and swept by again. People, sensing something extraordinary, were standing now as one, and with each pass a roar of *ole!* rang out.

El Cordobés was just warming up. He stood with his back to the bull and, still working next to the plank wall, passed the bull twice with his left hand. It was a wonderful bull, but it was surely approaching the time to kill him. El Cordobés, however, was no longer fighting as a mere mortal. He was working so closely to the bull that the front of his suit of lights was smeared with blood. Holding the *muleta* in one hand and wiping his long hair from his eyes with the other, he brought the bull back for another pass. The bull careened by and turned so sharply that what was actually two passes merged into one. *Ole!* The crowd was beside itself, wanting the fight to go on, but fearing that it would go on to a tragic ending. With the last close pass, the bull was hesitating just a little, doubting the reality of the *muleta* for the first time. Then El Cordobés—this time on his knees with his back to the bull—coaxed the bull into another pass; then another, coming swiftly back. With those two passes someone shouted out *"siete, ocho,"* tallying the passes. Surely, the matador was at the limit. *"Nueve"* came with El Cordobés standing again but not moving in a high *paseo de pecho* across the chest, and the crowd shouted *"diez"* as the bull tirelessly turned and passed again. Turned and slowly passed again. Turned and in ever slower motion passed again. Would it ever end? The plaza was delirious!

Finally, El Cordobés left the proximity of the red corral wall, to the relief and applause of the plaza, and walked toward the center of the ring. He stopped and called the bull, and the courageous beast came at the matador one more time. *Ole!* The bull turned, but did not pass again. It stood looking at the sweating matador, while blood streamed down its flanks. El Cordobés, quickly sighting along his sword, rushed at the bull and went in over the horns, thrusting the sword up to the hilt, high between the shoulder blades. Blood gushed from the mouth of the bull as he dropped to its knees as if shot. Deep relief and exultation swept through the plaza. The brass band struck up. Everyone stood and applauded and waved handkerchiefs as the matador saluted the arena. He was awarded two ears and a tail, and the aristocrats and the *aficionados* in the first few rows threw flowers and wine *botas* down into the ring. A mob of young Mexican youths got into the ring and carried the matador on its shoulders around the ring several times, then finally out the big door of the plaza to the passageways under the stadium. Everyone remained standing. No one left the plaza.

Corto "El Cordobés" las dos orejas y el rabo a un manso que se negó a embestirle. ¡Hasta que el le embistio! Y de una coridda gris, sin destellos brillantes, hizo una fiesta de entusiasmos elevados hasta la vertical del delirio. Había terminado, transcurran insensibles los minutos y el público permanecía en la plaza, contemplando al hombre tosco, que es sin embargo todo un monstruo de la torería.— Esto, *Mexico, D.F., Domingo 23 de Febrero de 1964.*

Canción del Cordobés

I. c. 1937

When the planes come
in the Mother Mary skies,
bombs pound the Loyalist village,
burst the stone and mud houses
of the hungry and poor,
sow murder in the maze
of old cobbled alleys.

Machine-guns hammer the workers' square,
hearts of peasant women hammer back,
a donkey catches fire in the marketplace;
a headless rooster runs
in ever-shrinking circles near the fountain.
Executioners prepare their blindfolds
(for half the village must be shot)
as the planes of Franco
twist like a knife for home.

II. c. 1937-9

The snot on the face of Manolo,
the hand of a nun that strokes it away.
A crust of bread and some acorn coffee
to keep the hunger pain away.
Wild cauliflower, a sort of thistle
to eat with a little ground meal.

There isn't any meat or olive oil
though Don Felix owns a herd of brave bulls
and the land that everyone works.

III. c. 1948

Under the light of the moon,
I will fight the bulls of Don Felix
in the lush pastures
across the Guadalquivir,
through the cold nights,
through the rain,
till the east is as red
as the blood on my hands.
A rough music we shall make;
the black bull swinging, rubbing
past my sister's tattered cape;
strum of my body on his flanks—
the two of us interwoven in a pasture plaza,
cheered by the crickets and the stars.

IV. c. 1954

Men of the Guardia Civil
have beaten me enough.
Jailed and banished,
my friend Juan and I,
must take to the road.
In the country we're like Gypsies

going anywhere to fight
anything resembling a bull.
Hitch-hiking, begging,
stealing a little fruit
from a fig or an orange
or an olive-ripe tree.
And always the special herbs
we pick to spread on our bleeding wounds,
burning the eucalyptus leaf to cure a cold;
fighting in forbidden pastures;
sleeping in frail huts and shacks of the poor;
eating grass like our four-legged brothers—
during this season of our souls.

      Fir nuts and acorns
      in my pockets—
      hopping the fish train to Madrid.

V. MADRID 1964

In the center of the ring
   here comes the bull.
I will pass him close as breath
     and spin him towards the wall.
Draw the *muleta* just before his eyes,
    and, like a cloud going over Toledo skies,
       the bull will pass.

Around and around
in the circle of the fight

with a flick of my wrist
the brave bull lifts
up and goes hooking
at the void.

I get high out there,
completely transcendent,
whirling the *muleta* past the death in his horns.
The people in their seats in the oval of the plaza
thunder one *Ole!* after another.

This is a pass for the early death of my mother,
and this pass I make for the stars.
This is a pass for dear Angelita,
and this for the cafes and bars.

O Brave Toro, come now to me,
this *corrida*'s a dream I have to be free.
The sticks in your back
clatter and brush me;
your darkness is all I can see.
Bless and forgive me
these moments with you,
the moment of truth
when you sense what I'll do
in front of these people,
the critics and fans,
the peasants and lovely rich ladies.

This is a pass, on my knees, for the Virgin.
Too close! This pass for our Spain.

This is a pass for the workers and farmers.
And this is a pass for the rain.

O Brave Toro, now you have caught me
and toss me high in the air.
I can't feel a thing, we're both on our knees,
the sand and our blood in my hair.

Not yet quite thirty,
I'm partially wealthy and
partially buried alive.

Hey, O Toro, we're just the same—
strong, wounded beings
caught by this Spain.

ELEGY FOR A LOG TRUCK DRIVER

Out the Sitkum River after a Week of Trail Work in the Bogachiel-Calawah Rainforest

—for Steve Conca

At the far end of the continent,
where the rainforest has been caught
and made to change its ways
to get the screaming saws
and log trucks through,
they're slapping another bridge
over the Calawah.

Moss and epiphytes will never grow
on a tree-farm Christmas tree;
and gravel roads and shiny metal culverts
supplant the largest spruce
and maples in the world.

Our pickup's from Japan,
our burro in the back
from the wild southwest—
we wait in the mud and rain
for the begrimed Indian flagman
to wave us through.

A whole side of a hill pulled down
for the road and bridge construction work.
What they do I don't know,
but the men in the muck and rain must toil,
and all this yellow steel and tractor-treaded-

Caterpillar-capital-invested-robot-
blue ox-mammoth American machinery
banging and roaring in the wind
would seem to know.

> *From deep in an ancient forest*
> *we enter*
> *the broken world.*

This mud, Steve,
in the rain our tires
whistle through:
gold of the land
we've turned to dross.

Down at the Mill

July 17, 1963

It's my first summer break from college and my first day down at the mill. I haven't worked in several weeks after getting laid off my previous summer job as a steward on the *MVS Coho*. Pulp & paper is to be, it looks like, my trade. First day, as I said, and I am nervous. On my way to report to the boss, I'm asking everyone, "Where's Mr. Flemming? Where's Mr. Flemming?" Flemming is leaning against a stack of plywood sheets, twirling a toothpick in his mouth, watching me wander around the shop looking for him. Finally, "Hey, kid," he calls, "who you lookin' for?" "Mr. Flemming, my boss." "Ain't no Mr. Flemming here, kid. My name's Flem."

So Flem gives me the word on what to do. He warns me of the dozen hazards of the beater room to which I am assigned. "If you happen to be cleanin' one of those machines and you're jammed down in 'em and the horns start blowin', get the hell out or you'll be newsprint tomorrow." A rather sensational way to make the headlines, I think. "Now get to work and don't let me catch you screwin' the dog," he adds.

July 18

Last night I worked in the beater room; today I'm catching planks that are tucked under bales of sulfide flaps shipped in old barges from Canada. Three jitneys unload the bales and I catch the planks under them before they hit the decking. I'm thinking it must be a little like longshoremen's work, which I'd like to try. Being green, I miss the first few planks and they go crashing all over the place—bouncing off a jitney or two and making nasty dents in their fenders. The foreman, Flem, ain't too pleased but he shrugs it off once I start improving. After a small pile of planks are built up, the crew and I drop over to the lunchroom for a cup of coffee.

Besides Flem and me there's the first jitney driver (he's the one in charge and wears a silver hardhat on a balding head), a second driver (fat and seemingly unimportant), and the third driver (he's young). One driver has a crane at home that everyone wants to borrow first day off. There's talk about home repairs, fixing fences on hog and chicken farms. The fifteen-minute break stretches to thirty.

"I told my wife," says the first jitney driver, "man, she's not goin' nowhere anymore with me when I step out 'cause the son of a bitch don't drink, and hell, every bit of cuttin' up I do gets crapped back on me the next day. I wouldn't mind if she'd smash herself up too. Boy, I told her no more unless she unloads herself as I do."

The others agree, "We know what you mean."

This is followed by silence, then more talk. Everybody begins complaining about their jobs. Silence. Then more talk about how everyone is getting screwed out of overtime. Then someone changes the subject, "During the war, I used to wait for those damn blackouts; then me and Big John—you remember that guy—well, every blackout we'd run in and cheek the ass of the waitress over in the cafeteria. Boy, what a tight ass. Wore a dress tighter than a fiddle string. Every blackout, you could hear comin' from the cafeteria, TWAAANG, TWAAANG, and that was me and Big John—you remember him—cheekin' her ass."

Laughter. Pause. More laughter.

Then someone says, "Ole Calvin's wife sure is a good dancer. Real smooth. You know what I mean."

Someone else, "Yeah, but I hear she's kind of a shaky Leo."

"Hey, that's what I hear, too."

"Ole Calvin sure is tight with the dough. I was out with him and his shaky Leo and I spent twenty bucks to his goddamn five. There was supposed to be a kitty where everybody kicks in the same. Bull shit! I got took. Is Calvin Jewish? After this, I go dutch or I don't go at all. One time he starts to reach for his wallet like he was going to pick up the tab, but see, he's real slow and by the time he would have gotten that damn wallet out, it would have been fucking-time. Yeah, he sure out fumbled me. That coon-faced SOB."

One of the men adds, "That puttin' in a kitty is no good anyway. Like me for instance. Hell, I drink beer all night while the other guys are chuggin' them mixed ones. Unfair!"

Everyone agrees. Unfair!

After a pause and serious reflection, a young guy with his lunch pail and gear comes in. He's got a missing finger on his right hand. Everybody knows him except me, of course. The crew kids him about how he can't beat off. He retorts that he isn't in love with his hand like some bastards he knows.

The youngest driver is reminded of a story about a kid who chopped off his finger in the woodshed. He ran into the house to tell his mother and his mother told him to run back to the wood shed and fetch his finger; but when the boy got there, he discovered that the dog had already eaten it.

This receives much laughter, followed by less interesting banter.

Back to work. The foreman pisses inside the barge; planks continue to get stacked; and after emptying twenty thousand dollars worth of sulfide stuff, we have just two bales to go when the shift whistle blows. Kazam! Everyone splits. I'm left with those two bales on the silent evening wharf. Some place, the mill, huh?

> Crown Zellerbach Mill
> Ediz Hook
> Port Angeles, Washington

Rainshadow Economics

1)

The treeplanters huddle
in the gypsy wooden camper,
playing Authors, drinking tea,
    dreaming sunshine
and a penny more per tree.

2)

The hand-loggers
    get their food stamps,
        buy the wine;
    the women bake dark bread
(maybe Joni Mitchell on
        battery-operated tapedecks).
pitchy, seasoned sticks
    of old Doug fir
    for cook-stoves
        and airtights
    in January.

3)

We check the high mountains for snow;
no snow yet.

Fenceposts split like light from a cedar log:
radiating wands from an orange sun,
warming horse-loggers' hearts
and the hearts of their women.

One dollar a post:
roughly seven inches per side, pie-shaped,
seven feet long, or within a wren's wing span.

The small ones we call California posts:
they can't be sure and they deserve to be punished
for their weird behavior.

The big ones, we call Washington posts
for the valley farmers
who have made alfalfa the foundation
for the mobile home.

They, too, deserve nothing better than California
posts, but they know the difference.

Kerouac Creek Work Tune

After three days of summer rain,
I'm back splitting cedar
                in the hills.
The horse skid-trail
                is muddy
            and rain clouds dapple
                        the peaks.

But work goes well,
        the saw and truck run fine;
        cedar splits
            into fifty
        sturdy rails,
        and by evening
        —truck loaded, tools packed away—

        the moon and stars
        jingle in the sky
            like wages.

Elegy for a Log Truck Driver

I know that swooping place
in the downhill curving grade,
after that volcano, Koma Kulshan,
skeets up like the moon
through the trees, after
a last thistled clear-cut
gives you the eagle's view
over Juan de Fuca waters
into Canada, distant mountains, into blue . . .

And there,
with your speed-splitter transmission,
king-of-the-woods heavy duty clutch,
high in your brand-new Western Star truck,
switching down through your gears
like a man dealing cards,
easing r.p.m. engine whine
with each bite of the brakes . . .

> "Maybe there is a way to get ahead
> in this cock-eyed land; have
> Vivian come home with the kids,
> build a little better place
> down by the river
> and have horses . . . "

BUT THE GODDMAN BRAKES ARE GONE

And the valves of your heart
thumped and fired like pistons

diving at your gears
trying to hold a dragon by its tail.

> "Last year, tested by the storm of recession,
> we prioritized our efforts, and as a result,
> cut our overhead costs,
> while maintaining our ability
> to serve the basic corporate needs."

Dragon of timber, dragon of steel,
plunging down a mountain road
with a tin-hat hero in your jaws.

> "Our profits are the primary
> determinant to add to our asset base."

O driver in the terrors
of the shadow of death,
free-wheeling past a last
thinned stand of fir—a
squirrel skittering out a
bough—snapping off a whanging
guard rail section, dispersing
rubber tread like shrapnel
in a long squeal of tires and smoke.

And then with the final curve
at the foot of the hill before you—
brain burning like a welder's torch—
you knew a way of escape:

"At the curve go straight
through the split-cedar fence
and on toward the river
through the fields;
then back onto Salmon Road,
or even left
along the river into wheat."

Out from the shadows of trees,
descending to the gentle river valley
with the seagulls dove-white in the sunshine
over the river like angels,
and the long trim pastures, sparsely
cattled, green vibrations in the heat.

That's when some extolling spirit
sprang into you heart,
as you began blessing farmers
for their lush fields of clover,

Jack Philips and Butterfly Pete,
who gave you your first chance to drive.

YOU REACHED THE CURVE

And the extolling spirit sprang again,
as you blessed without reason:

lumber executives
and their tennis-court wives,

caterpillar mechanics
in jumpsuits of grease,

drunken commissioners
and the builders of road.

YOU BURST THROUGH THAT SPLIT-CEDAR FENCE

And began blessing every which way:
hippies for their feminine hearts,
black men for their funny talk,

YOU PLOWED THROUGH THAT FIELD OF
FLEABANE AND CHICORY

blessing like a tickertape:
   union leaders
    suspenders
    squirrels
     women
      bar-tabs
      lice

    and the Lord;

   speeding toward the river like a curse.

But the irrigation stream—cool
sweet water of the Dungeness,
channeled off to a slow blue ditch

that gives the cows to drink
and the fields to ripen—

   you couldn't see it till you hit!

            The farm wife turns from her oven;
            the farmer looks out from the barn;
            a postman wavers by a mailbox;
            fishermen see fire in the trees.

Instant repeat gasoline explosions!

Forty crashing tons of you
bursting like a nightmare
above stunned waters,
clanging and crackling
      upward
higher than a man could ever bless,
         upward
            into ash-blossom
                whirlwind
            and the sun.

"When the Lord toucheth the hills, they smoke."

            And then, O Driver,
            you awakened
            on a hillside

            with a bird book
            in your hand.

BOOK TWO

BOOK TWO

Kuan-Yin Shan: Mother-of-Mercy Mountain

We also like blown cloud
*   across the face of the mountain. . .*
An old woman cooking
*   noodles for young soldiers*
*   in a makeshift wooden lean-to. A nice*
*   fire*

*   while fog-swirls dampen our sweaters.*

The summit's not far, a stone's throw
*   to the stone marker*
clear of razor grass (mang ts'ao) and cloud. And east
in descending veils: the rain—where the Strait should
be—then all the rest of China.

Kuan-yin, Bodhisattva of Compassion,
Kuan Shih-yin, Hearer of Cries; when
in trouble, she heals without question,
no credentials required.
Office hours: Eternal.

The washed-out rocky path
drops quickly; grass arches over
our heads. The path becomes trail
through bamboo and mulberry,
becomes road past tea farms
and grave sites,
rock quarries and oranges,

descending to the ferry town Pa-li,
where the water of the Tamsui broadens
before sweeping to the sea.
At the ferry landing, a shack
on pilings pours forth a smoke
black as the sand they're
sucking from the river bottom
and dumping in the bucket of a Cat.

    Then the river ferry comes,
    low in the rainbow oily water
    that reflects Kuan-yin.

REQUIEM FOR TIENANMEN SQUARE

The following translations were poems written by anonymous
Chinese involved in the Pro-Democracy Movement in China
during the spring of 1989 ("Beijing Spring"). The poems were
posted around Tienanmen Square, on walls and in under-
passes, in the days leading up to the massacre carried out by
the People's Liberation Army. The writings were gathered
from the Square and faxed to Hong Kong and then to the
Republic of China (Taiwan), where they were published
serially for many weeks in the *Chung-kuo shih-pao* [*China Times*].
Lo Ch'ing, a Taiwan poet and painter, then made a selection of
them and sought out foreign writers and poets—Korean,
Japanese, German, French and American—for translation.

我凝望

在廣場　我凝望

鮮豔的五星紅旗

四顆小星　已脫離了軌跡　因為那顆大星上

已塗滿了黃金

在廣場　我凝望

人民英雄紀念碑　走出來了　五四的先驅

因為偉大的愛國運動已開始

更加悲壯的故事

發生在這片多難的土地

在廣場　我凝望

雄偉的天安門

歷史在這裡重演

你為什麼總是沈默不語

數千萬的天之驕子啊

倒在你的胸前

你為什麼總是在這裡

導演一幕幕悲劇

I Am Watching

In the Square   I am watching
The bright red flag with the five stars
The four small stars   already off track   because
    the larger fifth star
has been smeared over with gold.

In the Square   I am watching
The commemorative stone monument of the people's heroes
    from whom was born   the May 4th vanguard
And because the great patriotic movement has already begun
There are so many more sad-brave stories
Unfolding in this calamitous land.

In the Square   I am watching
Majestic   Tienanmen
History here repeats itself
Why do you always appear silent?

Thousands of heaven's proud sons
Have fallen at your breast
Why are you always standing here
The director of tragic dramas?

今夜戒嚴

——歷史仍將由人民翻開嶄新的一頁

在共和國的天空下
今夜月朦朧
在共和國的天空下
夜晚已經降臨
但夜已不再黑暗
太陽已經照耀了二十個世紀
我依然感到寒冷
一條魚走上了甲板　被水手們好好捉弄了一番
他們正在向我射擊　我卻突然轉過身來
就用我肉體與靈魂的碎片恐嚇你們
這片無聲的土地足以毀盡我　我不願再生
月亮以一個輕鬆的手勢把我剖成兩半

我的頭顱裝滿了火藥
漸漸地向地平線上靠近
我翻起身起床　卻聽見
脚下一箇箇男人　還在沉睡
祇因為啊　她曾失去了太多陽光
你出來了　我出來了　他（她）也出來了
莫非　共和國的公民啊
這戒嚴之夜的空氣　溶入了這樣的芬芳
你的熱血　是在不屈的血管裡奔流的
今天　共和國的公民啊
你把他摔在了雙手上
洒下去　就是一片綠洲　是整箇民族的希望
這塊黃色的土地是我最初的摯愛

110

Tonight Martial Law Was Imposed, May 20

—But the people will still turn
a new page of history.

Under the republican sky
a hazy moon
under the republican sky
the fallen night
but it's no longer dark
the sun has shone for twenty centuries
though I still feel cold
a fish walking across the deck of a ship
is played such a good joke by the sailors
they are shooting right at me
but I suddenly spin round
use my body and soul like shrapnel to threaten them
this land of silence is enough to destroy me
I don't want to be reborn
the moon with an easy gesture
cuts me in half
my skull is filled with ammunition
moving gradually nearer the horizon
I turn my body and rise from bed
but hear under foot
men still drifting in sleep
you come out
I come out
he, she, also come out
is it possible, republican people,
that the night air of martial law is infused with fragrance

這塊黃色的土地是我最後的眠床

今夜　共和國的母親啊

我請求　躺在你的胸上

躺在這共和國的廣場

請賜我以力量　媽媽

請那輕浮般的戒嚴令

像細土般的滑落我年輕的肩膀

明晨　你會看到一個嶄新的朝陽

明晨　你的鬥志將更加高昂

在我的心裡

在您的頭上

共和國母親啊

自由和民主

那面光輝的旗幟　將高高的飄揚　飄揚

your blood flows in proud veins
today, you hold your future in your hands
sprinkles of rain, then there is oasis
the hope of everyone in the nation
this lump of yellow earth is my first concern
this lump of yellow earth is my last bed
tonight, I entreat you to lie face down
in the Square
may the frivolous ship of martial law
slide over my youthful shoulders as over fine sand
tomorrow morning you will see a new sun
tomorrow your fighting spirit will be greater
here in my heart and
there, above you
Freedom and Democracy,
that bright flag, will wave higher.

絕食

1·

旌——旗——飛——揚

希望中的絕望恰是絕望中的失望

絕食　絕食　絕食

從來沒有兩個字　像今天這樣

震動而有力

絕食是熱　溫暖土地溫暖禾苗

絕食是火　點燃標語點燃旗幟

絕食是電　擊傷麻木擊傷冷漠

絕食是雷　震憾血脈震憾心靈

絕食是風　掀起黑雲掀起希望

絕食是愛　愛我祖國愛我人民

絕食是恨　恨我貧窮恨我落後

絕食是愁　何時騰空何時崛起

絕食是怨　總是多災總是多難

2·

絕食是絕望的呼喊是最堅定的抗議

絕食是最脆弱的力量最頑強的鬥爭

絕食是光　穿透黑暗穿透夜晚

Hunger Strike, May 13

I.

Banners—flags—flying—spreading
Inside hope lives the seed of despair, and inside despair
   lives hope.
Fasting   fasting   fasting
There has never been a word   as strong as that word today.

II.

Fasting is a shout of despair, and the most unshakable protest
Fasting is the frailest power, and the most dogged struggle
Fasting is light   piercing the dark, piercing the night
Fasting is fire   lighting up slogans, lighting up banners
Fasting is thunder   jarring the bloodstream, jolting the heart
Fasting is wind   stirring up dark clouds, stirring up our people
Fasting is hatred   of our impoverishment and backwardness
Fasting is anxiety   when does it soar, from where
   abruptly arise
Fasting is ill-will   always fraught with disaster and calamity

III.

Behind me are the bones of the people's heroes
Commemorative stone guiding the ship of state
From the beginning of being   from the beginning of courage

3.

在它的后面，是人民英雄的骨骼

紀念碑是民族的航船的標誌

從生命開始　從英勇開始

從奉獻開始　從死亡開始

紀念碑默默地站在那裡

紀念碑警覺地站在人們的背後

提醒人們像它一樣沉著而堅定

每一次動搖

都會使民族的航船多一次迷惘

每一次動搖

都會使民族的航船多一些曲折

116

From the beginning of sacrifice to the gods   from the
    beginning of death
The monument has stood here in silence
The monument has vigilantly stood at the backs of the people
Every time there is a wavering
The ship of state becomes more bewildered
Every time there is a wavering
The ship of state pitches and rolls.

不要讓病中的母親聽見你淒楚的哭聲

不要凶殘的惡魔猙獰地狂笑

你不是看見母親的女兒都在奔走嗎?

那麼不要哭了,姑娘

高高地舉起你那綠色的募捐箱吧

看人民怎樣用正義和希望驅散烏雲

看人民怎樣和你年輕而美麗的心靈

一起歌唱

共和國的黃河淚已流得太多太多

但請你相信——

我們的民族不會衰弱我們的母親

不會死去

你聽那億萬行進的腳步聲

正敲響著——

中國民主

這新世紀苦難而美妙的樂章

Don't Cry

Don't cry, girl   don't cry
Our mother's ill, don't let her hear your sobs
Don't let evil laugh its obscene laugh
Haven't you seen that our mother's children are up and about?
Don't cry, girl
Hold your green collection-box high
See how the people, and you—the young and pure in spirit—
    sing together
The Yellow River of the Republic has flowed with too many tears
I only beg you to believe—
Our nation can't become weak, our mother can't die
Listen to the sound of a billion footsteps
Evoking Democratic China
This century like a discordant yet wondrous movement
    of a symphony.

五・二〇不眠的夜

這一夜軍隊開往北京

這一夜人民睜大了眼睛

這一夜一個真正的人民的將軍說：

誰敢對人民開槍，我首先打死誰

—— 題 記

五月的人民點燃了燎原的怪火

在這個最陰森可怖的夜晚

五月的共和國不再沈默

五月的共和國一直醒著

五月的政府一直醒著

五月的政權已在哆嗦

在這個强權與公理的審判庭上

五月的潮汐唱一支人民不死的歌

五月一直醒著　　五月不在沈默

站立在莊嚴國旗下的五月的

共產黨員啊

與夏夜的星星一樣多

May 20, A Night without Sleep

[On this one night, the army marched toward Beijing
and the people opened their eyes;
on this one night, a true general of the people said:
"Who dares to fire on the people will be the first I shoot!"]

The May Republic has always re-awakened
The May Republic will not be silenced
On this black night of threats
The May people have lighted a strange, uncontrollable fire.

The May Republic has always re-awakened
The May regime shivers against the cold
At this trial, brute force opposes justice
The evening and morning May tides sing
     a people who will not die
The May Republic has always recovered   it will no longer
     be silenced
Standing under solemn national flags,
the Communist Party members,
     now of May,
are as numerous as stars of the summer night.

小詰

孩子：媽媽，媽媽，這些小阿姨、小叔叔為什麼不吃飯？

母親：他們想得到一件美麗的禮物。

孩子：什麼禮物？

母親：自由。

孩子：誰給他們送這個美麗的禮物？

母親：自己。

孩子：媽媽，廣場上為什麼那麼多那麼多人？

母親：這是一個節日。

孩子：什麼節日？

母親：點火的節日。

孩子：火在哪裡？

母親：在每一個人的心靈。

孩子：媽媽，媽媽，救護車坐有誰？

母親：英雄。

孩子：英雄為什麼躺著？

母親：好讓後排的孩子看見。

孩子：是我嗎？

母親：是的。

孩子：看見什麼？

母親：七種顏色的花朵。

（作者是一個四歲的女孩和她的母親）

122

Small Questions

Child: Mama   Mama   these young aunties and uncles,
    why aren't they eating anything?
Mother: They wish to receive a beautiful gift.

Child: What gift?
Mother: Freedom

Child: Who will give them this beautiful gift?
Mother: They themselves.

Child: Mama   Mama   in the Square, why
    are there so many people?
Mother: It is a holiday.

Child: What holiday?
Mother: The holiday of lighting of the torch.

Child: Where is the torch?
Mother: Inside the hearts of us all.

Child: Why is the hero lying down?
Mother: To best let the child behind him see.

Child: Am I that child?
Mother: Yes.

Child: To see what?
Mother: The flower with petals every color of the rainbow.

中國

他的手又開始蠢蠢地活動

把我的腿鋸下來　把我的頭拋向刑場

那些孩子們仍在教室裡呼吸

無數辦公室的門打開又關上

選民一致通過　聊天看報喝茶

這群奴隸早已現代化了

我的自由被沒收　鎖在衣櫃裡　和內褲一起發霉

而被月亮殺死的古典詩人

再不敢醒來

太陽突然發狂　我已經無路可逃

人群密密麻麻　高速公路通向四方

一直把我逼進單人房間　恐懼

置身於歷史英雄的嚎叫黑夜

給自己輸氧穿緊身衣

百葉窗縮回來　排遣我罪惡的處境

我的四肢換成了不鏽鋼管　被他們擦得乾乾淨淨

我的眼睛瞎了　挖出來像瓶塞　與廢紙一起飄浮

空虛層層壘壘　它是我每天敲打的飯碗和木筷

China

His hand again begins to prepare for attack
Amputating my legs to the groin   throwing my head
   to the execution grounds
The children still breathe in schoolrooms
Numberless office doors open and close
Those with a vote share a consensus   chat, read newspapers,
   drink tea
These slaves were already modernized, early
My freedom has been stolen   locked in a clothes closet
   with mildew and underwear
And the classic poet has been killed by the moon
and dares not rise again.

The sun suddenly goes mad   already there is no road
   for my escape
The people crowd tightly together
the freeways flow in four directions
Directly, I am forced to enter a single hotel room   FEAR
I am placed in the black night where history's heroes
   scream
Give myself oxygen, strap on a straitjacket
The venetian blinds recoil   take comfort in my evil
   plight.

My four limbs become stainless-steel tubes   wiped
   so clean by them
My eyes are blinded   plucked out like corks   afloat
   with the wastepaper

不可否認　黑夜來了

我不能偽造星星　敷衍我的軀體

那無法縫合的傷口和黎明

我的臉不是農民的臉與這土地卻有共同的形態

廣場陷落了　在南方　我投宿於下等的旅館

街頭的海腥味使我作嘔

我眞想與市民們一起死去

126

Layer upon layer of emptiness   this is my daily
    knocking of rice bowl and chopsticks
Unquestionably   the black night has come
I cannot build the stars   or deal perfunctorily with my body,
That wound and the dawn which cannot be healed
My face is not the face of a farmer, but it has
    the same resemblance to the land
The Square fell to the enemy   in the south   I stayed
    overnight in a cheap hotel
The smell of seafood in the streets made me sick
I wish I had died with the citizens.

贈言 — 給 XN

這個城市没有太陽

黑夜繁殖蟲 和蛆

一具僵硬的屍體 掙扎著歪斜

企圖支撐這裡的天空

幸運的人是蛆 不幸的人是石頭

在幸與不幸之間

在石頭與耗子之間

祇有你才明白 它是什麼意味

Words for XN

There is no sun in this city
Black night breeds maggots and worms
One body in *rigor mortis*   struggles to right itself
The lucky people are rats   the unlucky, stones
Between the lucky and the unlucky
Between the stones and the rats
Only you can understand   what it means.

瘋　女　人

整日躲在中國的盒子裡洗嬰兒的尿片　幾千年了

現在　我把自己的肉體攤開

捶成金屬的刀子　劃破這箇世界的嘴臉

這些男人的嘴臉

中國　一箇殺死了自己的兒子的父親

在這夜裡又凌辱他的女兒　中國　中國

一口活棺材　我白白地陪葬了你們幾千年

我的雙乳　變成了我自己的墳墓

周身長滿了霉菌一樣的苔蘚

這箇國度僵屍氾濫　我的赤裸的身子浸泡在

膿血般　流淌的黃河和長江上　幾千年了

它們洗不白我的皮膚

我躺在床上　嗚咽地撫摸自己蹂躪自己

中國　那些一本正經的男人總是令我失望

幾千年了　只有我一箇人從這口活棺材裡爬出來

摒棄了無處不在的無聊和死亡　打破了黑暗

我黑眼睛　黑頭髮　黑色的衣裙

黑色的脚　還有黑色的黑色的靈魂

但是我的手套是白色的

這一雙白色的手能夠殺死我們的父親

我是中國一箇歇斯底里的女人

第一箇瘋女人那又怎麼樣

在深更半夜裡　我從家裡　跑出來

才撇開了自己的丈夫

Mad Woman

All day long hidden in the box called China
   washing diapers   for thousands of years
Now   I spread apart my own bones and flesh
Beat them into a metal knife
slash the disgusting faces of this world
The disgusting faces of these men.

China   a father who killed his own sons
And this night, molested his daughters   China   China
A living coffin   in which I have been buried
   for a thousand years
My breasts   have become my own tomb
The whole length of my body
grown over with lichen and moss.

Corpses overflow this nation   My naked body soaks in
The pus and blood   flowing thick on the Yellow and
   Yangtze Rivers   for thousands of years
They cannot wash white my skin
I lie in bed   weeping and caressing myself, abusing myself
China   These proper and respectable men always disappoint me.

In thousands of years   only I, one person, have climbed
   out of this living coffin
Abandoning the pervading boredom and death   smashing
   the darkness

My black eyes   black hair   black-colored skirt and blouse

那又怎麼樣

我是瘋女人　脫得一絲不掛

站在樹上尋找著太陽

在所有男人們的會議上　我是投反對票

那又怎麼樣

過地農民的國度

過地小市民的國度

過地官僚的國度

他們從無數次戰爭

從幾千年的歷史和時間中仍沒有得到拯救

在死亡的轉角處　在與土地的結構中

他們從奴隸到奴隸

那些曾反方向扭動的手臂終於撓帘般垂落下來

變成了植物

建立在謊言之下的報紙

與建立在灰爐之上的長城是同一的

文質彬彬的學者　不願下葬的老人

與那些滿不在乎的青年是同一的

蹲在公廁的著名的詩人與電腦化的孩子是同一的

星羅棋布的茶館與那些辦公室研究所是同一的

我憎恨一切　孔子　莊子　斯大林　馬克斯

他們使我作嘔　我要吞下所有的欺騙和罪惡

Black-feet   and black, black soul
Only my gloves are white
This one pair of white gloves can be enough to kill our father.
I am an hysterical Chinese woman
The first mad woman   but so what
In the midnight hour   I run away from home
Casting off my own husband
But so what.

I am a mad woman   not a stitch of clothing on
Standing in a treetop, searching for the sun
At the places where men vote   I am the opposing ballot
But so what.

Throughout the land the nation's farmers
The nation's small-town people
And the bureaucrats
have come from innumerable wars
From thousands of years of history, and in so much time
  have not been rescued
At the intersection of death   in the earth's anatomy
They have gone from slavery to slavery
Their arms, once wrenched counter-clockwise, finally drop
  like roll-curtains
And change into plants.

Newspapers founded on lies
And the Great Wall founded on ashes are the same
Refined and gentle scholars   old men reluctant to be buried
And the insouciant, I-don't-give-a-damn young men are the same

我死了　我羽化了　而我卻不能神話般地奔向月亮

中國的　骯髒的　用星星紋身的夜

又奸夫似的　趴在我的肩上

羞辱了我的情人　我要殺死你

從此　你再也不能玷污我的身體

我不是瘋女人　我是人　我甘願受到懲罰

Famous poets squatting in public johns and the computer kids
   are the same
Tea houses, spread out and numerous as stars, and the offices
   of research institutes are the same
I hate everything   Confucius   Chuang-tzu   Stalin   Marx
They make me sick   I want to swallow all falsehood and crime
I died   I took flight   and couldn't race toward
   the moon of immortality
The filthy China night   body tattooed with stars
Like an adulterous man   lies face downward on my shoulders
Humiliating my lover   I want to kill you
From now on   you can't pollute my body
I am not a mad woman   I'm a human being   and am willing
   to suffer my punishment.

Japanese Currents

Stone steps strewn with blossoms;
Rain rinsing tile roofs.
"Cherry blossoms should be viewed at night,"
Said Mr. Yakomoto to his Chinese tutor.
And Mei-hua ran out of the theater
When the "Japs" in the movie
Bombed the Mainland school.

Tour buses, tourists made in Japan,
Pass endlessly on Chungcheng Road
To and from the mountain park
Where at the end of Occupation,
As the story goes,
They released all the snakes from their labs.

Wooden houses, tatamis and the way
To do tea.

In the early century a systematic
Extermination of the headhunting natives
Reduced the tribes to a docile photogenic flock,
A mountain people who once lived
Beside the sea.

Unpainted wooden houses, wood-paper screens
And the way
To do flowers.

"Toyota isn't negotiating sincerely—"
The United Daily News.
"And how about all these Taipei girls
Wearing that nurse-like hose?"
"It's big fashion in Tokyo."

They knew how to tap sulfur springs
For tile indoor baths,
And their trade surplus stupendously grows.

"Some preferred the Japanese education—"
A Taiwanese landlord.
"China will never sing company songs—"
A Mainlander boss.

Blossoms scattered in the rain on steep
And narrow steps.
And the Shingyo I chant every dawn.

YANG-MING MOUNTAIN
Taiwan

Setting Out
by Tung Nien, Chapter 46
   —translated from the Chinese

(SCENE: TAIWAN, 1960)

Li-li's maternal grandmother had been telling a series of
interesting stories, but finally it was she, not Li-li, who fell
asleep. The noisy snoring of Li-li's grandfather nearby and
the croaking of the field frogs in the night made him restless.
The air was also humid and stuffy. Several times Li-li looked
out the dark window, unable to stop imagining that the
wavering shadows of trees might be evil spirits. Then, trem-
bling and holding his breath a moment, he was certain he saw
a black shape at the window screen. He was petrified.

The shadowy image faintly cried, "Ma-oom, ma-oom." At the
same time, Li-li heard a motorcycle moving fast on the road
from the village. The black image suddenly withdrew from
the window. Li-li thought he heard dogs begin barking about
the same time. In a little while, he began to relax, and soon
he became drowsy and fell asleep.

He rolled over in bed several times and finally opened his
eyes. Earlier, his sleep had been disturbed by a flock of small
birds flying from the ridge of the roof to the courtyard
bamboo. From the window he watched them swoop up and
down, then hop and dance in the branches and leaves. The
bright sky also seemed to shine into his clouded heart. He
sighed deeply and finally came from behind the curtain of the
old bed.

The sun had already risen above the rooftop, and beyond the backyard wall it was burning brilliantly. Because of this, the shade within the wall appeared just that much deeper and cooler. Several women around the well were preparing and arranging chickens, ducks, fruit, and vegetables. These reunited sisters, other relatives, and friends talked of old times as they worked. Their conversation was frequently enlivened with laughter. A small circle of men nearby were smoking and discussing affairs of the nation. Every so often one of them, with hardened face, would express his views, gesturing dramatically, causing raised eyebrows and sidelong glances. Such passion went against the grain of the leisurely discussions.

"Here's Li-li," Grandmother announced. "It's my darling daughter's son."

The women all gave their attention to the boy. He stood on the railing of the back gate, keeping his gaze on the brick well. From below the ground, the spring water gushed up through a hollow bamboo tube to just above the water level of the well. Through the blue-green surface ripples, dense patches of algae, growing on the inside walls of the well, were visible.

"At last you are awake. I can give you some chicken soup and rice congee for breakfast," Li-li's grandmother said, washing her hands and standing up. "Today I'll be very busy worshiping at the temple. I won't have much time to look after you."

As Li-li's grandmother spoke, gongs and drums began sounding beyond the village at the site of the religious ceremonies.

"Last night, a . . . ," Li-li began. "Last night there was something like a ghost, Grandma."

"What ghost?" his grandmother said. "Shhhh. You don't want to scare people."

"Your story, you didn't finish it and fell asleep. I . . . there was a shadowy figure at the window crying, 'Ma-oom, ma-oom.' When it finished moaning, it ran away."

"Ma-oom, ma-oom," repeated the grandmother, looking furtively about. "This ghost business, you don't want to mention it again. It can frighten people. If anyone asks, don't say anything. There's no reason to think it was a ghost. You just dreamed it in your sleep. Relax now and eat your breakfast."

Li-li convinced himself that he must have dreamed or imagined it and, feeling somewhat relieved, began to eat his breakfast. On further thought, however, he felt that his grandmother had reacted a little too nervously. She had darted out past the backyard to where the field path reached the trees. She was now standing there looking in all directions.

After breakfast, Li-li ran to the same spot in the field to take a look. But in the huge fields, he could see only a stream flowing through the landscape and, on its banks, dense bamboo groves. In the field was also a raised mound which was the air-raid shelter.

"What are you looking at, Li-li," asked Little Uncle.

This uncle was still a child. He had climbed high into a guava tree to pick the fruit. Several boys and girls, holding bamboo hats to catch the guavas, waited beneath the tree, their necks craned upward.

"Do you want to come down, Little Uncle?" Li-li asked. "I have something I want to tell you."

"Okay, I'll just pick a few more and then come down," Little Uncle responded. "Do you want one?"

"I don't want one," Li-li said, looking out again past the trees to the fields and the gray, obscure mound of the air-raid shelter covered with thick grass.

"What are you looking at?" Little Uncle asked, sliding down the tree.

Li-li led his uncle away from the trees into the field path, then he said, "Last night I saw a ghost."

"What? You're kidding."

"No, honest. There was a black figure outside my window, crying, `Ma-oom, ma-oom.'"

"Crying what?"

"Ma-oom."

"Crying Mamma?" Little Uncle asked. "And afterward?"

"The dogs barked and it ran away," Li-li said. "Grandma said I only imagined it, but as soon as I told her, she ran out to look at the air-raid shelter. Don't you think it's strange?"

"Do you want me to keep this a secret? We can't just tell anyone," Little Uncle said, looking quickly around.

About noon, several policemen came to the village. The local country folk—both men and women—poured tea and offered cigarettes, while those who had returned from the city, or who were college students, stood around looking angry.

"The Ministry of the Interior's vice minister is a relative of mine," a college student said with a hint of provocation.

"Yes, yes, we know this," one policeman said. "We are here only to carry out a little government business. We just want to take a look around, that's all, merely take a look around."

"But if we find who we're looking for, we're still going to arrest him," another policeman said. "The relative of the vice minister can do what he likes, but sedition is still sedition. Last night someone saw him at the bus station."

"Perhaps they were mistaken," Li-li's grandfather said indignantly. Then, out of their hearing, he added, "Such despicable yes-men."

"Everyone does their best, Grandpa," said Li-li's grand-mother. Then she turned to the policemen and smiled, "If he returns, I certainly will tell him to surrender. These young people are naive; they don't understand these things."

"'Don't understand these things?'" the grandfather said. "You have a weak brain, woman! If they don't understand these things, how can they pass the college exams?"

"All right, Grandpa, don't get angry," said the son of the county government secretary. "It's a holiday. Won't you gentlemen celebrate a bit with us? Please stay and have something to drink."

"No, no. We have to be off," said the policeman in charge. "Sorry to have disturbed you, sorry."

From the direction of the village, the drums and gongs of the religious ceremony from Royal Palace Temple continued to reverberate. Soon, the sound of shrill horns lifted the music higher. But even though the atmosphere of the celebration for the good harvest was beginning to permeate the mood of the local people, and even though the noon meal of wine and complementary dishes was now ready to be served, nothing could extinguish Grandfather's indignation and bitterness. On the contrary, the wine supper made him and a number of other people even more irritated.

"What kind of a world is this anyway? What kind of real justice is there?" said an employee of a paper-making factory, his face flushed with anger. "You people who can be logical, listen to me. Before, because we are Chinese, we risked everything to get the Japanese out. Now that the Japanese have left, must we struggle against occupation by the mainland Chinese?"

"Taro is taro," said the grandfather. "A sweet potato is a sweet potato. The mainland Chinese are mainlanders; we Taiwanese are Taiwanese."

But at the mention of Japan, several youths—some sober, some drunk—began to sing a Japanese martial song, overpowering the conversation.

"This is a tragedy. This is the kind of tragedy you get from China's defeat in the war," one professor said with emotion. "Am I right?"

"I'm not too clear about your meaning, but it's certainly a breach of etiquette, Professor," Li-li's Third Uncle said. Then, a little pompously, he added, "When a nation suffers defeat in war, it is even more reason that it should create a serious political, social, and educational system that is competitive with other nations. If a nation can't be serious about these things, the consequences are sure to be tragic."

"When you say tragic, you mean sad," a local youth said bitterly. "My situation is tragic. All I did was speak out against privilege, against terror by those in power, and against corruption. The school dismissed me, goddamn it. With such bad luck, I haven't been able to do anything or go anywhere since. I pass my time wandering the fields. My family is overworked like water buffalo. This, my friends, is tragic."

"You still have had some good luck," the professor said. "No one has said you are a Communist. And you still have the accumulated merit of your ancestors."

As they talked back and forth, someone turned again to the subject of the police search.

"If there was anyone at the bus station who saw Ah-ch'ing, then Ah-ch'ing ought to have come back last night," said one of the group. "The person I saw was the wrong man."

"That boy, Ah-ch'ing, doesn't know where to hide."

"He better not come back here," Grandfather said angrily. "A person like him who doesn't study, gets involved in politics for nothing, loves to talk—if he comes back and runs into me, why, he'll get a poke in the mouth and his legs broken. I can do it."

"Li-li," Grandmother said. "Come here, if you're finished eating. You can help me. Go with me to the temple to worship. Do some of you others want to go now?"

A number of women immediately said yes. One great aunt instructed Li-li, "All small children must go to worship. Then, when they grow up, they will become good scholars."

The group carried thank-you baskets full of the prepared chicken, duck, fish, beef, vegetables, fruit, and sweet cakes. With an air of piety, they walked off across the fields of cut rice. Only stubble, chaff, and spilt grain remained where they walked. The high sun shone golden on the open fields. Gleaning birds formed flocks there and flitted about on the ground. At intervals, near the front of the temple, a string of firecrackers suddenly flashed and exploded in the air.

The small temple was located beneath a banyan tree at a crossroads. Being located among the fields, the temple was not often frequented. But now, persons from all corners of the village passed in an endless procession, trailing clouds of incense.

Presently, across the road from the temple, the empty stage for thanking the gods with offerings became loud with the thunder of drums announcing the start of the folk-opera show.

Grandmother took Li-li's hand in hers and stopped at the roadside. "Li-li, do you remember the ghost last night?"

"Uh-huh," he said. "Was it Uncle Ah-ch'ing?"

"Oh, so you know? Yes, he's hiding in the air-raid shelter. Wait until there are no people about and give him this money."

"Do you want him to come back and help eat the offerings?"

"I want him to hide a little farther away," Grandmother said. "Tell him I said he's not to come back again."

"I understand," Li-li said. "Tell him not to come back again."

A Bow to You, Bu-wen

Your small form
("petite" in any other context)
in saffron-colored robe,
hair cropped, a watch
and rosary loose upon your wrist . . .

I taught you English
from Reps, Shunryu Suzuki
in the zazen hall each day.

"I decided to be a nun,"
you said, "when my parents
arranged my marriage. I
was already a Buddhist."

At zazen, I never heard
or saw you move an inch;
and was impressed
by how a sitting Asian
looks just like a Buddha.

"I know I'm not a monk,"
I told you, "but as Suzuki
saw it, we Americans
are something else than laymen."

"I think I understand that, but
we," you said, "are Asians."

I often pictured you with hair
grown out, and wearing jeans,
the two of us hiking about
in mountains in Korea.

Then you fell ill. Poor nutrition?
Too little sleep? So on a visit
I said, "Why not drop out? Go
to the university, do zazen
and just cut loose the rest."

You smiled (you had that capacity,
whatever came) and said,
"In Korea, my temple, my
order, is very poor, severe,
and my Master wants me back."

What could I say? So I simply
left it, for love or
for lack of conviction,
or respect or fear of your tradition.

Later, I saw you on the street.
You'd taken the vows—the four scars
burned by incense on the foretop
of your head. "Bu-wen," I exclaimed,
"so long since I've seen you."

Not far from the temple, we
were on opposite sides
of a street vendor's wares.

It was awkward to talk. You called
my name. But we didn't say anything
in the way we had
in summer heat and autumn cool
of the zazen hall, before.

WHEN THE TIGER WEEPS

(Translations from T'ang China)

For a Buddhist Monk
—*Chia Tao (779-843)*

In a tangle of mountains,
in autumn trees, a cave—
hidden within,
a magic dragon pearl.

Poplar and cassia
overlook a blue sea;
rare fragrances waft
from a stone pagoda.

A monk since young,
you still have no white hair;
you enter upon meditation,
in a frost-streaked robe.

Here there is no talk
of the world's affairs—
those matters that make
wild the hearts of men.

贈　僧

亂山秋木穴裡有靈蛇藏

楊桂臨滄海石樓聞異香

出塵頭未白入定衲凝霜

莫話五湖事令人心慾狂

賈島

Looking for Immortals
—*Chang Chi (776-c.829)*

At the stream's source,
the path leads on
to gray cliffs.

Everywhere,
among blossoming apricot trees,
dwell Immortals.

A hermit says,
"More can be found
on West Peak,

and two or three
have their home
in the clouds."

尋仙

溪頭一徑入青崖處處仙居隔杏花
更見峰西幽客說雲中猶有兩三家

張籍

Fasting Taoist Woman, Residing in Mountains
—Chang Chi (776-c. 829)

Stillness, stillness
in the flowering branches—
at the thatched hut,
swept strings of a zither.

Because you're now in mountains,
the way you see has changed;
when meeting visitors,
you do not speak your heart.

The moon rises
on the quiet river road;
cranes cry from trees
deep in cloud.

If I could learn
the art of alchemy;
I, too, would settle
in an unknown wood.

不食仙姑山房

張籍

寂寂花枝裡草堂唯素琴因山曾改眼見客不言心

月出溪路靜鶴鳴雲樹深丹砂如可學便欲住幽林

Looking for Ts'ui Cheng, Recluse of Lu Mountain
—Ch'iu Wei (c. eighth century)

With the sun high,
the dog and chickens are at rest;
the gate is shut
against the cold pond.

In the evening,
bamboo almost hides your hut;
the fall garden chills
a stone bed.

You've already lived
years on this mountain,
taking elixirs
for a long, healthy life.

When those who pretend
to have left the floating life
encounter you,
it only adds to their pain.

尋盧山崔徵君

邱為

住山年已遠服藥壽偏長虛棄浮生者相逢益自傷

日高雞犬靜門掩向寒塘夜竹深茅宇秋亭冷石床

Looking for, but Not Finding, the Recluse of West Peak

—Ch'iu Wei (c. eighth century)

On the mountaintop:
one thatched hut, ten miles from roads.
Knock on the door:
no disciple to answer;
look in: only a table for tea.

The firewood cart is covered;
have you gone fishing
in the autumn stream?
I look among the pools,
but miss you; I try but fail
to pay my respects.

Grass shines in the fresh rain;
pines murmur at evening windows.
Here at this moment a harmony,
profound and unrivaled;
the self completely cleansed,
the heart, the ear.

Although there is no guest
or host as such, I'm able to intuit
your pure thought.
Purpose fulfilled,
I head back down the mountain—
no need now to wait for you.

尋西山隱者不遇

邱為

絕頂一茅茨直上三十里扣關無僮僕窺室唯案几

若非巾柴車應是釣秋水差池不相見黽勉空仰止

草色新雨中松聲晚窗裡及茲契幽絕自足蕩心耳

雖無賓主意頗得清淨理興盡方下山何必待之子

161

Reclusion, Late Summer

—Yao Ho (fl. 831)

To this place of retreat,
the world does not follow;
but many old ailments
heal here.

I polish words
of old poems;
view mountains,
and sleep outside my hut.

Colored clouds
cross the setting sun;
cicadas whine
in leaves of trees.

With this,
my heart again knows happiness;
and who would have thought,
without wine or money?

閒居晚夏

姚合

閒居無事擾舊病亦多痊選字詩中老看山屋外眠

片霞侵落日繁葉咽鳴蟬對此心還樂誰知乏酒錢

Taoist Master in Mountains
—*Chia Tao (779-843)*

You've brushed your hair
a thousand strokes,
but your gaunt face shows
you've stopped eating grain.

You raise crane chicks
to full maturity,
plant seeds
to grow tall pines.

A Taoist concoction simmers
through the night;
a cold stream pounds
through the day.

Never far from this
secluded place,
you're lost
to the people of the world.

山中道士　　賈島

頭髮梳千下休糧帶瘦容養雛成大鶴種子作高松

白石通宵煮寒泉盡日舂不曾離隱處那得世人逢

A Chung-nan Mountain Monk

—Kuan-hsiu (832-912)

The voice of success and profit
may stir the vault of heaven,
but not this place.

In the rounds of the day,
you wear threadbare clothing
and eat simple fare.

When the mountain snow deepens,
your thoughts
are far from those of men.

Occasionally,
Immortals pass your door
and knock.

終南僧　　　　　貫休

聲利掀天竟不聞草衣木食度朝昏

遙思山雪深一丈時有仙人來打門

Farewell to a Palace Lady Entering the Way
—Chang Chi (776–c. 829)

In the old Han Emperor's
Chao-yang Palace,
a woman most rare
sought to make Immortal.

Her name originally stood out
in palace records;
she was not yet accustomed
to robes of colored clouds.

But she stopped
singing and dancing (both much praised)
and long followed
the flight of the crane.

Officials of the Court
stood by as she entered a mountain cave;
then drove the jade-wheeled car
home empty.

送宮人入道

舊寵昭陽裡尋仙此最稀名初出宮籍身未稱霞衣
已別歌舞貴長隨鸞鶴飛中官看入洞空駕玉輪歸

張籍

The Monk's Room, Shu-ku Monastery
—Ch'i-chi (864-937)

At a place deep
in green trees,
a lamp's light
burns long.

Spring pilgrims
make their way to the temple;
blossoms fall
at a monk's closed gate.

In the mind,
the ten thousand doctrines are still;
a clear, lone spring
swirls over rocks.

We do not ask
about our lives, our work,
and the silence between us
we keep.

書古寺僧房

綠樹深深處長明焰焰燈春時遊寺客花落閉門僧

萬法心中寂孤泉石上澄勞生莫相問喧默不相應

齊己

From the Courtyard—for Monk Ju-hsien
—*Chiao-jan (730-799)*

I view the colored peaks
incised upon the autumn sky,
listen to the pine grove
in the calm of night.

A lone figure
hasn't been seen for some time,
practicing the Way
in snowy clouds.

秋居法華寺下院望高峰贈如獻上人　皎然

峰色秋天見松聲靜夜聞影孤長不出行道在寒雲

Ling-ling Temple

—Hsieh Ling-chih (fl. Early eighth century)

He stays in a thatched hut
in Ling Mountain Valley;
studies diligently by oil lamp
the *Odes* and *History*.

In this still world without people,
his rustic door's half-shut;
only white clouds go with him
through the night.

靈巖寺　　　　　　　薛令之

草堂棲在靈山谷勤苦詩書向燈燭

柴門半掩寂無人惟有白雲相伴宿

Mourning the Death of Ch'an Master Tsung-mi
—*Chia Tao (779-843)*

The trail is dangerous
among snowy, silent peaks.
With the Master gone,
who goes this way to meditation?

Dust slowly gathers
on the tea table;
before his death,
tree colors already had changed.

The pagoda stands
in blowing pines;
footprints fade
along the roaring stream.

Passing by the grieving temple,
the tiger
hears the sutra,
weeps.

哭宗密禪師

鳥道雪岑巔師亡誰去禪几塵增滅後樹色改生前
層塔當松吹殘蹤傍野泉唯嗟聽經虎時到壞菴邊

Sakura

Lingering at door of bathhouse,
I watch the woman bundle off children
into light-rain, small-lane Kyoto.

Skirt in hand, she glances
my way across the evening road,
then up the walk after the party
of colored rain boots and umbrellas.

Wet-headed but warm, I'm waiting
for Ling-hui, to come out from the public bath,
but can't help thinking of America,
the disquietude strangers there inspire.

Cherry trees are just beginning to break
blossom, here, off Kitaoji-dori, north of town.

Now the woman is crossing the lane,
coming directly toward me. She wants
to give me her open umbrella,
insists that I take it

without knowing where I'm going
or who in the world I am.

I thank her and bow,
and point to my broadbrimmed hat.

Am I sure, she implores, am I sure?

There's hardly a raindrop
in the rain-freshened air.

She smiles and bows,
returns to the sliding doors of her house.

Kyoto, the old capital,
bursts into blossom in my heart.

Notes to the Texts

NOTES TO "Song of Ishi"

"Song of Ishi" is a poem cycle derived from Theodora Kroeber's book: *Ishi In Two Worlds*. Gary Snyder has referred to Ishi as " . . . surely the patron Bodhisattva of our Northern California nation . . ." or, of any place, really, where civilization encroaches on wilderness.

"Ishie Shantie" is a Chinook Jargon rendering of the cycle's title poem, "Song of Ishi." The English and Chinook Jargon have a line-by-line correspondence.

Waganupa is the same mountain known today as Lassen in Northern California.

Special thanks to poet Don Jordan, Cheyenne Nation.

"Song of Ishi" is for Michael Daley.

NOTES TO "Canción del Cordobés"

The best biography of El Cordobés is still *Or I'll Dress You in Mourning: the Story of El Cordobés and the New Spain He Stands for* by Larry Collins and Dominique Lapierre (Simon & Schuster, 1968).

"Canción del Cordobés" is for Shannon Gentry.

NOTES TO "Requiem for Tienanmen Square"

I made an initial English translation of several of the Tienanmen poems in Taipei with assistance from Taipei Associated Press reporter, Annie Huang, immediately following the military crackdown. These were for publication in English-language newspapers, such as Taipei's *China News*, and several magazines in Asia. A revised version was later forwarded to intellectual circles in America for public presentation, and Jack Estes, an authority on popular culture, videotaped a Peninsula College faculty reading of the poems for public television. Poet Bill Slaughter, a former resident of Beijing, also made the poems a part of his public-reading repertoire and later included several in an essay for his book *The Politics of My Heart*. Further small-press publication included Bob and Susan Arnold's *Longhouse*, and the Pacific Northwest's *Crosscurrents*.

On my return from Taiwan for a visit in 1991, I again revised the translations for publication in such journals as *Bombay Gin*, *Chicago Review* and *International Quarterly*.

I was surprised and greatly encouraged to see how these utterances from Tienanmen Square provoked so much interest in America, and how they came to life in our culture. Clearly this was due to the sympathetic chord the events of Tienanmen Square struck in people who value freedom, and with those who suffer political oppression. I think it also connected in a special way with many who recalled the Vietnam War protests during the sixties and early seventies.

Wang Wei, a scholar and Chinese dissident, who, like many others, fled China in the aftermath of the military repression, was extremely helpful in clearing up difficulties in the translations, as well as in assuring me of the continued relevance of the poems, despite more than a decade's passing. As an indication of the degree of danger that surrounded those who took part in the Chinese protest movement, the authorship of these poems, even among dissident and exiled parties, remains either unknown, or secret.

The late poet and human-rights activist Allen Ginsberg, while still teaching at Naropa University, was kind enough to look over these translations. He said he had heard about them and was eager to read them. He referred to them as "action poems" and commented that "historically the poems are exciting, and poetically, medium exciting." He noted the reverse Marxist jargon of some of the poems. Aside from the issue of how much poetry I have lost in translation, I myself have come to think of these verses as documentary poetry. I recall that they were written under harrowing circumstances, and what they may lack in aesthetic polish can be forgiven for what their existential immediacy brings to our conscience.

Printing these poems here, fifteen years since the debacle, is still timely if one believes in the perniciousness of what Fang Li-chih—"China's Sakharov"—identifies as the authoritarian "technique of forgetting history"; and timely too, considering the several hundred so-called "forgotten prisoners"—workers, students, teachers and farmers—who vegetate in China's jails, all indicted for "crimes" related to activities of the protest movement. Some two thousand students and their supporters in Beijing were believed to have been killed when the military moved against them, but evidence was deliberately destroyed by the soldiers, so no accurate count could ever be made.

Shortly after the crackdown, the government's propaganda machine announced that no one had been wounded at Tienanmen Square.

"Small Questions"— From a dialogue between a four-year-old girl and her mother. The "rainbow flower" is a flower in a child's cartoon series on Chinese televison; the flower has magical properties and is considered highly auspicious.

NOTES TO "Setting Out"

Tung Nien, the pen name of Ch'en Sun-shin, is the author of numerous short story collections and novels, including the prize-winning *The Bodhisattva of Pen Yuan Temple*, whose protagonist is the the young hero of *Setting Out*. Tung Nien lives in Taipei with his wife and children.

NOTES TO "When the Tiger Weeps"

"For a Buddhist Monk"—Chia Tao
The *magic dragon pearl* is a symbol of enlightenment. Depending on the variant characters in the texts of Chia Tao's poems—and there are many—

one could translate any number of lines differently. The first two lines of the second stanza, for instance, could be translated (rather flatly): "A Buddhist staff / hangs from an overlook to the sea." The last two lines are possibly related to Verse 12 of Lao Tzu's *Tao-te-ching*. In the Chinese text, *Wu-hu* (Five Lakes) is the name of *T'ai-hu* (Lake T'ai) located on the borders of Kiangsu and Chekiang Provinces, but it could also be shorthand for "five lakes, four seas," meaning all of China, ergo, the world. In any case, the *affairs of Five Lakes* are not—whatever else they may be—the talk of these mountain recluses.

"Looking for Immortals"—Chang Chi
West Peak here is likely the West Peak of sacred *Hua-shan* (Hua Mountain), in ancient times a mountain known for its hermit caves. *Immortals* (hsien) can refer to mythological beings, shaman-poets, or Taoists, who attained immortality. In this poem, however, the word refers to a self-realized or enlightened individual, or sage, who may be Taoist, Buddhist, a mixture of the two, or non-denominational. The character *hsien* (Immortal) also was used as we use it, namely, as a synonym for "great," as in "an immortal writer."

"Fasting Taoist Woman, Residing in Mountains"—Chang Chi
Tan (cinnabar) is the Chinese character used here that signals alchemy. In Taoist alchemy the mineral cinnabar, containing mercury, was the major substance for preparing elixirs thought to confer immortality.

"Looking for Ts'ui Cheng, Recluse of Lu Mountain"—Ch'iu Wei
Lu Mountain occupies some one hundred and sixty square miles of northern Kiangsi Province. It is famous for its highly changeable cover of clouds and mists. Just to the southwest of the mountain is the native place of the great poet of rustic reclusion, Tao Yuan-ming (365-427). The *floating life (fu-sheng)* has numerous connotations, but here it is a reference to a life of superfluities and ephemeralness. *Stone bed (shih-chuang)* refers to a stone platform or bench that was used for sleeping and meditation. It was standard furniture for many hermits.

"Reclusion, Late Summer"—Yao Ho
Yao Ho was a poet who occupied relatively high official positions. From

time to time, influenced by seclusion-loving poet-friends, such as Chia Tao and Wu-k'o, he sought out places of retreat.

"Taoist Master in Mountains"—Chia Tao
The act of brushing one's hair suggests both daily ritual and a concern for grooming despite the retreat to wilderness. *Taoist concoction* (literally "white rocks") is the fare of recluses. In translating, I chose the word *concoction* to hint at alchemy and/or pharmacology, which included minerals as well as herbs.

"A Chung-nan Mountain Monk"—Kuan-hsiu
The Chung-nan Mountains divide north and south China, running east and west some fifteen miles south of the capital Ch'ang-an (today's Xian). The mountains were the haven for China's shamans-turned-hermits during the early civilizing period of the country. Later, by T'ang times, the mountains had become the place of retreat for large numbers of people, including Buddhists and Taoists and intellectuals, i.e. scholar-officials who might be developing interest in either Buddhism or Taoism, or might simply be following the time-honored Confucian tradition of choosing personal virtue over public office.

"Farewell to a Palace Lady Entering the Way"—Chang Chi
The *Han Dynasty* (206 B.C.-A.D. 7); the Later Han Dynasty (25-220). *Colored clouds* refer to Taoist religious attire. The *crane* is a symbol of immortality. *Jade-wheeled (yu-lun)* is a synecdoche for "imperial carriage."

"The Monk's Room, Shu-ku Monastery"—Ch'i-chi
The *ten thousand doctrines (wan-fa)* is a reference to religious rules, pre-cepts, principles, etc., that can be in some instances as entangling to a monk seeking enlightenment as the *ten thousand affairs (wan-shih)* or *ten thousand things (wan-wu)* of the material world.

"Mourning the Death of Ch'an Master Tsung-mi"—Chia Tao
Master Kuei-feng Tsung-mi (780-841) was the Fifth Patriarch of the Hua-yen (Flower Garland) school of Ch'an (known later in Japan as Kegon). This school emphasized the *Avatamsaka Sutra (Flower Garland Sutra)*, an important Mahayana scripture said to be the only teaching expounded by the Buddha during his enlightenment.

Mike O'Connor is a poet and a translator of Chinese literature. A native son of the Olympic Peninsula, Washington State, he spent more than a decade farming in the Dungeness-Sequim River Valley and cedar logging and tree-planting in the Olympic Mountains. From 1979 until 1995, he lived mostly in the Republic of China, Taiwan, studying Chinese language and culture while working as a journalist. An MFA graduate of the Jack Kerouac School, Naropa University, and a recipient of a literature fellowship from the National Endowment for the Arts, he currently resides with his wife Liu Ling-hui, a dance teacher and choreographer, in Port Townsend, Washington. *When the Tiger Weeps* is his eighth book.

How We Got Our Name:

from *Pleasure Boat Studio,*
an essay written by Ouyang Xiu,
Song Dynasty poet, essayist, and scholar
(January 25, 1043)

"If one is not anxious for profit, even at the risk of danger, or is not convicted of a crime and forced to embark; rather, if one has a favorable breeze and gentle seas and is able to rest comfortably on a pillow and mat, sailing several hundred miles in a single day, then is boat travel not enjoyable? Of course, I have no time for such diversions. But since 'pleasure boat' is the designation of boats used for such pastimes, I have now adopted it as the name of my studio. Is there anything wrong with that?"

—Translated by Ronald Egan